MW01630806

Thunder in the Night

A Sailor's Perspective on Vietnam

Ray Kopp

BP

Brundage Publishing

Thunder in the Night

A Sailor's Perspective on Vietnam

by

Ray Kopp

BRUNDAGE PUBLISHING
Room 203 Executive Office Building
33 West State Street
Binghamton, NY 13901

www.brundagepublishing.com

Jacket design by Amanda Nord

Library of Congress
Control Number: 2004113587

ISBN Number: 1-892451-28-X

Printed in the United States of America

Dedication

This book is dedicated to the memories of my nephew SPC-4 Brian Dale Upright, my twenty shipmates who died on October 1, 1972, and the rest of the 58,000 United States service members who died in the Vietnam War.

God bless them for their efforts and God Bless America.

SPC-4 Brian Upright, 1970

Acknowledgements

I want to give a special thanks to Chuck Zendner and the staff of the *USS Newport News* (CA-148) website, without whose work I never would have been able to do all the research and information gathering I did in writing this book.

Thank you to Brundage Publishing for their exceptional cooperation and expertise in making this project professional and fulfilling for me. Thanks to Franklin Resseguie, Barrie Hoople, Jennifer Sembler, Rachel Edwards, and Amanda Nord.

I would like to give credit for the photographs to the publishers of the *USS Newport News* 1972 Cruise Book, Walworth Publishing Company. I would also like to give credit to Scott Mason and Ed Hale.

Thank you to Stephen Mogck for his exceptional work painting the author's portrait.

Thank you to all who helped in the creation and publication of this book.

Preface

Within the general public, the topic of war creates disunity crossing religious, ethnic, cultural, generational, and political boundaries. The question of whether or not war is necessary, along with deep concerns whether such measures are morally correct cause protests, rallies, sit-ins, and walkouts. It is, however, generally believed by this same arguing public that within the military there is a deep feeling of brotherhood across the four military branches. This has become more prevalent in the years since my experiences in the Vietnam Era. There is much more inter-service unity today.

As a Vietnam Navy veteran who served on a large ship, I have experienced criticism from some veterans. I have been disrespected and disenfranchised by groups of veterans and non-veterans alike. Some believe those who served on ships in the Navy have no claim to being true combat veterans. Their belief is that unless you experience "real combat" (meaning in-country, on the ground combat), you have not experienced the realities of warfare. The most common image of warfare in Vietnam is that of the foot soldier on the ground. For many of those same veterans, the air war and the sea-borne assaults hundred of miles to the north and in the final stages of the war did not exist. It was not a part of their experience in Southeast Asia. It is also worthy of note that for many who were stationed "in-country," combat was never a part of their experience.

I am sure this book will draw its own degree of flak from those who question my story, but I will stand my ground regardless of what my detractors may say. Every service man or woman involved in combat—whether at sea, in the air, or on land—forever feels the affects of that experience in their life.

It is my hope in writing this book that all may see one facet of the Vietnam War from a new perspective and realize that—in any war—no soldier, sailor, or airman serves without peril, anxiety, sacrifice, and life-long consequences.

Thunder

The voice radio call-signs of military units vary greatly. Some are mundane and uninspiring; some are overly intellectual or refer to terms from the romance classics. Some denote Greek or Roman heroes, heroines, or mystical gods. More often than not, many seem inappropriate and dissimilar to the functions or appearance of the items to which they are attached.

The heavy cruiser *USS Newport News* (CA-148) came from an era of mighty warships that had given way to a modern Navy of aircraft and missiles. She was commissioned after the end of the Second World War, and had been designed to carry the might and power of the American Navy to its enemies with fast and furious power. Somehow she was appropriately assigned the call-sign "Thunder," and from the perspective of those who witnessed her fury from a distance, it must surely have seemed an accurate moniker.

To us it was a matter of great pride.

USS Newport News CA-148

Table of Contents

Chapter 1

Reminiscing on *USS Newport News*

"We're going right into the tiger's mouth Ray, as far north into Vietnam as you can go, right near the Chinese border. I'm scared shitless, man!"

"Where, Hanoi? Where are we going?"

"Haiphong."

"Where is Haiphong?"

"It's the biggest port city in Vietnam, about twenty miles east of Hanoi; it's where all the supplies and munitions come in to North Vietnam from Russia and China."

"Holy Shit!" Ray's eyes widened as he tried to keep his voice down. "Gung Ho, motherfucker, we're gonna go kick Charlie's ass."

"Screw that," Dave said, "there are Russian and Chinese ships there. It's the most heavily defended place in North Vietnam, and they have hundreds of 130 and 155mm cannons and missiles. Not only that, Seventh Fleet has been seeding the harbor with mines since last week."

"Yeah, but our guns shoot nearly twenty miles. We won't even see the place; we'll be over the horizon."

"No, that's just it, some of the targets are inland between Haiphong and Hanoi. We have to get within a couple of miles of the shore to hit them. Also, there is an intended psychological effect they're trying to achieve. They want to do it right in Charlie's face, up close and personal. It's nuts!"

"Dave, don't worry. Do you really think the U.S. Government is going to put a big heavy cruiser in a place where it could be sunk or disabled in enemy territory? There must be more to it than that. They must know something you don't."

"Listen to me! It's not just us either. COMSEVENTHFLT is going to be on the *Oklahoma City,* and the *USS Providence* and two destroyers, the *Buchanan* and *Hanson*, are going in as well."

Ray let the words sink in and thought for a few seconds before speaking again. "Calm down buddy, the Navy is not going to risk three thousand men in one operation! There must be other stuff here that you don't know about, it can't be that risky."

"I'm telling you Ray, I've been in the Off-line Crypto Room with Lieutenant Eisenhower for the last two days. I've seen all of it. They call it a strike plan. First, there are naval gunfire strikes, then the mines are supposed to be activated after we leave the harbor to barricade future shipping. The messages are all Top Secret OEO. I'm technically not even supposed to be there, but we don't have enough TS cleared officers with crypto training to handle all the message traffic. If Eisenhower knew I was telling you this I'd be in a world of shit, so you have to give me your word you won't say anything. I mean it."

"Hey, you know me. We have an agreement—nothing goes anywhere, but I think you're worrying too much."

"Maybe, but I know what I've seen, and it looks like craziness to me. I just had to tell somebody, I can't keep it to myself."

"Well what does Eisenhower say about it"?

"Shit, you know him, he wouldn't say shit if he had a mouth full of it."

* * *

Eight days earlier, on May 1, 1972, two sailors sat playing guitars in the ladder well connecting Radio One to the main deck aboard the heavy cruiser *USS Newport News*. Playing music on their acoustic guitars was one of several ways to while away their off-duty hours. Their mood was pensive; their thoughts had been streaming continuously for nineteen days since leaving Norfolk, Virginia. The entire crew knew that things were changing rapidly. They all felt excitement and apprehension when they heard new information about their unexpected deployment.

So far, Ray's Navy career had been comfortable; it was indeed an enjoyable adventure for the twenty-year-old. Coming from a rural farming region in northeast Pennsylvania and being suddenly thrown into this world of international travel, high tech information systems, and Cold War military culture had already been an incredible journey. He found moments of intrigue and occasions of great pride. The awareness that his government entrusted him with information and resources at the highest levels of national security had become a badge of honor to Ray. There were also opportunities to embrace the cultures of what, to his young mind, seemed to be other worlds.

His thoughts wandered as he and Swanny played melodic chords and soothing rhythms. Images of warm Caribbean nights, sunny days SCUBA diving in St. Thomas, bright autumn afternoons in Northern Europe, and sandy beaches on the Virginia shore came to Ray's mind. He also remembered cold stormy nights in the North Atlantic, boot camp and technical training in San Diego, and the flight to Guantanimo Bay where he had reported aboard *USS Newport News* two years earlier.

For two years the ship had been his home, and she was a beautiful one as Navy ships go. She was a monument to a by-gone era, but one that had been well preserved and continually upgraded. She represented the high point of Naval artillery technology and possessed a massive firepower capability. However, guns were considered relics of the past in this modern world, and the focus of Naval weaponry was now on aircraft carriers, jet aircraft and missile launching surface craft, and submarines. In the post World War II years most remaining gun cruisers in the Navy's inventory had been converted to missile cruisers with rear turrets removed and launchers installed in their place. Many newer ships had no guns onboard-this was to be the trend of the future.

Despite this trend, *Newport News* was an icon. The last of only three Des Moines class cruisers designed in the final years of World War II, *Newport News* was commissioned in 1949 and spent most of the 1950s and 1960s in the Second and Sixth Fleets plying the waters of the Atlantic and Mediterranean. In 1962 she had been updated to serve as a fleet flagship. She was a showboat. Terms like "spit and polish," "boot camp," and "by the book," applied to life aboard *Newport News*. She had a proud history that included being the flagship of Second Fleet during the Cuban Missile Crisis and two tours in the Vietnam War.

As Second Fleet flagship, the capacity in which she had most recently served, *Newport News* was a mobile and capable platform. COMSECONDFLEET, in military lingo, was the commander in charge of U.S. Naval Forces Atlantic, Commander NATO Forces Atlantic, and Commander Joint Task Force 122 (a multi-service Caribbean task force).

Newport News was the only all-gun cruiser left in the U.S. Navy, and was the largest gunship afloat. The Iowa class battleships of Uncle Sam's reserve fleet had been "mothballed" in 1969 with the decommissioning of the *USS New Jersey*. These ships awaited future activation should they be needed, but had been negotiated away in the political war by fervent outcries from the North Vietnamese over the destructive power of the battleships. *Newport News* could only be outgunned by the Iowa class battleship and, technically speaking, only in terms of main battery armament and the number of secondary battery guns.

Forward main battery guns, USS Newport News

The Iowa class battleships were armed with a main battery of three triple turrets, but these were manually loaded guns. They could only fire eighteen to twenty shells per minute. Each shell had about the destructive power of a 2,000 pound aerial bomb; what was referred to as a blockbuster for its ability to devastate an area approximately the size of an average city block.

The nine rapid-fire, auto-loading guns of *Newport News'* main battery could fire ten shells per minute each, giving the cruiser a firing rate of ninety shells per minute from her main battery of guns. Added to the much faster rate of fire was the ability of these smaller weapons to be quickly re-aimed to fire at more targets in a much shorter time frame. They shot eight-inch projectiles, which had the destructive effect of a 500-pound bomb. The greater number and ability to strike more targets, however, made them as effective as the battleships in some cases. Secondary batteries for both the battleships and heavy cruisers consisted of five-inch twin mounts; the battleships having twelve of these, or twenty-four guns, while the heavy cruisers possessed six, or twelve guns). Finally, both types of ships had an array of three-inch twin mounts.

Cruisers were fast and maneuverable, had a shallower draft, and could engage more targets. Battleships were twice as wide in beam and nearly three times the weight, making them much deeper in draft, heavier, and thus slower to maneuver.

Ray had always been interested in military hardware, especially aircraft and naval vessels. Several members of his family had served in the Army, Air Force, and Navy as officers and enlisted men. Ray's brother Arthur had served in the Navy during the Korean War. While Ray's Uncle Nelson, his mom's older brother, had been one of his idols since early childhood. Uncle Nelson had retired as an Air Force colonel in the late 1960s. Ray's mother had often updated him on the lives of Nelson and his three sons who followed him into the officer ranks of the Army and Air Force. It was the colonel's presence at Ray's boot camp graduation in San Diego that had been a source of great pride. Later at dinner with Uncle Nelson and Aunt May, Ray's lifelong hero had spoken words that, to Ray, represented a rite of passage into adulthood. "Son, I know you're going to be a damn good sailor. I hope you can come to LA and visit us while you're here in California."

Ray's early memories were imbued with images of the brass buttons and gold filigree of West Point uniforms handed down for him to play with. Like many children of the 1950s, Ray's awareness of all things military was stirred by the Cold War culture in which the archenemy of the United States was the threatening, communist Bear of the Soviet Union, and, to a lesser degree, Communist China. In his first years of primary education "duck and cover" was a very real part of his life. Air raid drills were routine in grammar school. The civil defense authorities had mounted an air raid siren atop his father's farm machinery business and a large aviation navigation aid was painted on its roof. He often watched the B-36s, B-47s, and B-52s of the Strategic Air Command as they flew high altitude training missions over rural Pennsylvania. Most people in the area did not notice, but rarely did Ray miss anything that flew. Had he grown up near a military base or seaport, he would have noticed details of those environments, but in the rural farmlands where he lived, the major government presence was the continual readiness training that went on miles above the landscape.

By the mid-1960s much of this aviation activity had subsided. Apparently, the Air Force had switched its training venue to other locations. The air raid drills of earlier times had also faded away. Missiles and rockets became the new focus of Ray's military consciousness. Through his high school years he kept up with advances in weaponry and Aerospace technology. The Cuban Missile Crisis in October of 1962 both frightened Ray and spurred his curiosity about strategic weapons systems. He had an unquenchable thirst for information and read everything he could on these topics. He was shocked as he struggled to comprehend the massive destructive potential of these systems.

With adolescence came a divergence of interest from the military and technical to the biological, social, and sexual. When superpower saber rattling eased and his interests meandered, it was time to explore the more pleasurable aspects of life. But there were periods when his concerns were peaked by the specter of war once again. At first, Vietnam was a nondescript thing, not even a declared war, and not particularly threatening. It crept slowly into the collective consciousness of the time. Was it a police action? A conflict? A skirmish? In the mid-1960s it was hard to define. As time went by new terms surfaced: the domino effect, commandos, guerrilla warfare, Green Berets, firefight, and Viet Cong. It all seemed surreal to Ray.

His family had always watched the nightly news; it was a family ritual that coincided with the evening meal served on TV trays. It served as the information hour for the family, keeping them apprised of current events. As they watched the news, Ray found that more and more time was being allotted to a tiny country in Southeast Asia. On the other side of the world American soldiers, with a smattering of loosely coalesced "free world" forces, were fighting against…what?

The stance of the U.S. Government and the Johnson administration suggested the U.S. was fighting Communism, an agenda its citizens had been conditioned over decades to accept. But there was very little knowledge among the general populace of a Communist threat in Southeast Asia. Moreover, most U.S. citizens had never even heard of Vietnam. Where was it, and how important was it really to the security of the United States and the rest of the free world?

No answers were forthcoming. American military "advisors" had been lending technical support and training to South Vietnam for years now, but actual combat involving U.S. troops, if it existed, was not acknowledged. Then came the Tonkin Gulf incident in August of 1964, where two U.S. Navy destroyers, the *USS Turner Joy* and *USS Maddox*, were fired upon by North Vietnamese torpedo boats. This flashpoint led to the Tonkin Gulf Resolution, the start of American Forces involvement, and the escalation of direct military activity.

Four years later, the Tet Offensive by the Communist North in January 1968 brought Vietnam to the forefront of world events. Suddenly, the news media was flooded with footage of real combat. The major television networks began covering the events in Vietnam and soon had expanded their evening news programs to a full hour to focus on them.

By the late '60s, Ray and his male friends became aware that the serious business of war was likely to play a part in their future. The selective service had been re-instituted and young men were being drafted. A new wave of patriotism swept the youth of the time, bolstered by older generations who assured them that the United States did not undertake warfare without just cause and careful consideration. The feeling prevailed that if we, as a nation, were engaged in fighting for freedom in some foreign land, there must be good reason to do so, even if that reason was unclear. Enlistment in the military rose as patriotic youths followed the example of Americans who had gone to war in earlier times.

For Ray personally, it was never a question of *if* he would serve, but rather *where* he would serve; which branch of the military was perfect for him. Following his interests, it seemed like Air Force, Navy, Army, then Marines would have been the logical order of preference. At times, social interaction with his friends rearranged this order. The topic became more prominent to all the boys as their high school years drew to a close.

Ray's best friend and life-long cohort was his nephew. Brian. They were the same age and had shared much of their upbringing in a relationship like that of brothers. Brian was the son of Ray's oldest sister Virginia, the second oldest of Ray's four siblings who were separated by a span of twenty years. Hence, Ray's oldest brother Art and sister Virginia were grown and raising families of their own when Ray and Brian were born in 1951. The two boys were inseparable and had a genuine kinship of mind and spirit. "Soul mates" would not have been an inappropriate term to describe the kindred spirit of Ray and Brian. Both boys being patriotic, in their final years of high school they often talked of joining the service together. The "buddy system" was a recruiting term of the time, initiated for the purpose of keeping good friends together in military service. But, in the end, their interests diverged and Brian chose the Army while Ray decided on the Navy. In their senior year both enlisted, each in their chosen branch.

Ray was a strong swimmer and had become interested in SCUBA diving with an interest of becoming a "frogman." Spurred on by the Navy recruiter, he had applied for specialized training in a program known then as UDT, Underwater Demolition Teams. The prospect of becoming a Navy diver and working with explosives excited Ray, but as his Navy training unfolded, it became obvious that the military used well-established methods of determining the talents an individual possessed and adjusting his career goals to meet the needs of the service. As a result, Ray's training was redirected toward the realm of radio communications and he was assigned to the communications engineering crew of *USS Newport News*. He had become quite comfortable with this occupation.

* * *

These were the things Ray thought about as he sat with Swanny, playing music and contemplating the moment. These were the ideas and events that had brought him to this point, somewhere in the Pacific Ocean on May 1, 1972.

The two sailors finished their session and quietly packed their guitars back into their cases. They placed their instruments back in Radio One and then took their usual evening stroll about the main deck. It was 10:00 p.m., and there would be little to do for the remainder of this day; perhaps another hour or two of relaxation and contemplation, then sleep.

Chapter 2

Steaming Toward Vietnam

The night was clear and dark, and the stars shone brilliantly as Swanny and Ray stepped from the hatchway onto the main deck. It was a comfortable sixty-five degrees with low humidity. There was no wind except what was created by the ship's movement. Faint reflections on the mirror-like ocean surface shimmered in the distance. Closer to the hull, the sea rushed by until it became engorged in the propulsion system near the stern of the ship. They walked toward the fantail where the ship's four massive propellers churned the sea into a white, frothy rooster-tail of incredible thrust. As they continued farther back the sound and vibration became a crescendo beneath their feet. *Newport News* had been averaging twenty-eight knots, twenty-four hours a day, for all but two of the last nineteen days.

They strolled forward, and several minutes later found themselves nearing the bow of the ship. It was impressive to stand on the manicured teak wood timbers of her main deck and feel the relative wind created in this placid environment. At the bow, a spray of smaller proportions appeared effervescent in the dim moonlight. The only sounds were the hissing of wind, the whirring of the water flowing by, and the din of the electrical and mechanical equipment that always accompanies this ghostly gray giant. She was capable of thirty-three knots at flank speed, but cruising continually at twenty-eight inspired a certain sense of awe. Crewmembers here and there walked, smoked, talked, and relaxed on the multi-level weather decks, but the soft, tan, teak planking of the spacious main deck was by far the most comfortable aspect of this 717-foot leviathan. The teak seemed to take away the harshness and coldness of the steel of which the ship was constructed.

Newport News was a home on the sea to the 1,100 men who lived within this floating community, solitary in its presence as it made good speed toward its next assignment. It was not unusual for this crew to know the solitude of solo cruising. *Newport News* was a stand-alone element. The concept of the cruiser class of ships was a Naval tradition originating with the clipper ships during the American Revolution and they were solo men o' war, meant to be self-sufficient. The concept was that the cruiser class was heavily armed to out-gun anything smaller than itself and fast enough to out-run anything larger. They were the raiders of the high seas, often acting alone, but also capable of coordinating resources with other fleet elements.

As Ray and Swanny took in the natural beauty of this warm night, Ray's thoughts again wandered. Their training during this transit period was much more rigorous than anything they had yet experienced. Earlier that day, the medical corps personnel (corpsmen in Navy lingo) had presented a session comprising several hours of combat first aid training for a group of about twenty men in the CR division berthing quarters. Topics included life saving and first aid, and these had been both practical and graphic, complete with simulated injuries and discussions of emergency treatment methods. It had been both informative and alarming. As they stood at the edge of the deck gazing into the clear night and smoking cigarettes, Ray turned to Swanny:

"God Swanny, do you believe that first aid class we had today?"

"No, I don't know what to think. It was amazing, you'd think we were going into serious combat the way they were talking—how to perform a tracheotomy, sucking chest wounds, severe burns, CPR!"

"I couldn't believe what the guy was saying about pissing on exposed intestines?"

"No, I couldn't imagine that, but I guess it makes sense. His point was that in a gaping abdominal wound one of the greatest concerns, after loss of blood, is to prevent the exposed internal organs from drying out and dying. It's important to keep them hydrated right?"

"Right, and if nothing else is available, urine is a last resort. He did say that urine as it leaves the body is fairly clean, but I found the whole thing, I mean covering these things in such detail…what the fuck!"

"Well, remember, there are only about ten medical staff on board for 1,100 men. It's like everything else we've been going over recently, they're concerned with trying to prepare us for the worst case scenario, don't you think?"

"Yeah, right, but I mean, what are the chances? We could have a fire, that's always the greatest concern at sea, or an ammo explosion; I can see how those things might produce those kinds of wounds. The fire fighting and damage control is routine training, but in the past two years I've never seen it this intense or specific."

"Well, you know the government Ray: train, train, train. It's a good thing I'm sure, and we *are* going to a war zone. It's not like it's going to be a pleasure cruise, but I guess the ship's been there twice before without casualties."

"Yeah, and I don't think there's really any naval surface warfare there. The cruisers and destroyers just sit off shore and lob shells to support the grunts, from what I know. Besides, we're supposed to be pulling out of Vietnam, turning it over to the gooks, right? I mean it doesn't look like there's much left to be done at this point. We'll probably shoot a few rounds here and there and go back to Second Fleet, they're saying six months max for this deployment."

"I don't know Ray. Dave was saying some of the intelligence reports and other stuff he's seen are saying the North Vietnamese have mounted a major offensive, and there's a lot of shit happening right now. COMSEVENTHFLT made an urgent request for major caliber naval guns in order to get us over there. What do you think that means?'

"I think it's just because the battleships are no longer in commission. They need a gunship to support the ground war, and we're it. From talking to MacMullin, Hect, and Wilcox, the '69 WestPac cruise was fairly low key."

"Wilcox, Hect! Yeah, those guys were pretty cool. I wonder what they're all doing now as civilians."

"Lots of partying and getting laid I'll bet. They probably have hair down to their asses by now; nobody can even tell they were ever in the service. That's the only way you get laid in the U.S. these days, you know. Anybody with a military haircut is a piece of shit, right?"

"Yeah, what's that about? Christ, why are they blaming us? We're just doing our duty, fulfilling our military obligation. It's not like we want war; we're serving our country. They didn't reject our fathers and uncles in World War II. They supported them, respected them."

"Times are different now, Swan, the whole world is against this war. I think it's all because of communist propaganda; the Reds have convinced everybody that the U.S. is the great aggressor, the warmongers trying to take over the world. And here we are, supposedly in the Age of Aquarius. Our generation believes peace and love are what life is all about. We're supposed to have evolved beyond violence; there shouldn't be any more wars, etc. etc. How can you argue with that? It's a noble concept, it should be true."

"Yeah, true, but is it real?"

"I don't know. I try to believe it, but I also have a patriotic side that says we should be willing to support democracy and freedom, it's what the U.S. has always stood for."

"Exactly. Don't you think the communists would take over the world if we didn't oppose them? You know what the scene is like in Europe. Remember Finland, Norway, and the other Scandinavian countries we visited last year? Those people loved us because we were on the other side. They're scared to death of Soviet aggression."

"Interesting they were the only places we've never been demonstrated against. Too bad our own people can't feel that way, we'd have a chance in society instead of being treated like assholes by our own peers."

"It's just the ignorant ones Ray. The down to earth people like Cynthia don't buy that shit. She's behind all of us. There are a lot of others too; they have the same values as us and they believe we're right."

"Yeah, Cynthia, she's a great little lady Swan, I'm lucky to have her. Too bad all young women don't have their stuff together like that; she's not going to be dragged into any of this hippie, druggie, craziness bullshit. Bless her little heart."

"Right! Hey buddy, it's 12:30, I need to get some rack time. Let's head back to the compartment."

"Yeah, me too, 6:00 comes pretty early these days. I'm still trying to get used to this port and starboard watch schedule, twelve hours a day. It'll take a while to get adjusted."

* * *

Ray lay in his bunk, the closest to the floor of three "racks" in a row of twelve tightly spaced bunks which made up one-fifth of the beds in the CR division berthing compartment. As he drifted to sleep in the red hue of the battle lamps, memories of his past entered his thoughts once again.

Ray still felt great sorrow when he thought of Brian. The autumn of 1970 brought tragedy to his world. It wasn't the first time he had encountered death, but Brian was the closest person he had known who had died in the war, and the loss was unimaginable. It was personal, and it was unacceptable. His mind still reeled when those memories found their way into his consciousness, and this was one of those times.

The image came back to him unexpectedly. It was a brisk fall day with puffy clouds and rustling leaves. The chill in the air depicted the ominous approach of winter. About one hundred people had made their way to the cemetery, listened to the interment prayer, and watched the coffin descend silently into the green earth as the honor guard folded and presented the nation's flag to Ray's sister, Gina. Strains of the popular song "The Green, Green Grass of Home" filtered through the scene in his mind. All was quiet as the group contemplated their final moments in the presence of Specialist Fourth Class, Brian Dale Upright. And then the sudden, piercing burst of seven rifles firing the first of three salvos of the 21-gun salute. They were all taken off guard. Ray remembered the shrieks that burst forth involuntarily from his sister and Brian's beloved Mary Pat; the emotional release was totally uncontrolled. Many looked around in great surprise as the second and third volleys followed. As their nerves calmed and the expressions of shock subsided, tears burst forth from many eyes. It was over.

How could it be true? How could that have really happened to Brian? I still feel like I will wake up some day and find it was just a nightmare, he thought.

For most people not directly involved in it, the Vietnam War was far away. In 1972 it seemed the world in general let Vietnam fade from its collective reality. The media frenzy that held everyone's attention during the great and protracted escalation in the late 1960s had waned to a monotonous background murmur. America was weary of Vietnam; the record had not been a good one. Civil unrest and societal currents in this country and abroad had brought about a strong desire among the masses to get America out of the war. To that end, the will of the majority was driving political energies. The process known as "Vietnamization of the war" had been implemented—U.S. ground forces were being pulled back and sent home. The focus had changed to enabling the South Vietnamese to carry on their own defense.

U.S. military forces fought in the skies and coastal waters in Southeast Asia, and special operations units were involved on the ground in certain areas, but the taking and holding of territory by foot soldiers had largely been given over to the Army and Marines of the Republic of Vietnam. The United States was willing to supply and support their fight against the Communist aggressor to the north, but popular opinion had turned against the commitment to continue efforts regardless of the cost. This was hard for Ray to reconcile in light of Brian's death. What was it all about? What was it for? Thousands of young American lives, like Brian's, lost, for what? Now we were pulling out? How could that be? The question repeated in his mind as sleep came upon him.

* * *

Ray awoke as revile sounded over the 1MC. Precisely at 6:00 a.m., as always, the voice came bursting forth: "Now revile, revile, all hands turn to and begin the daily routine. All officers to quarters and prepare for morning muster. Set the underway watch detail, breakfast is now being served on the mess decks. Now revile." The compartment night-watchman made his rounds, shaking the sleeping sailors to make sure each was awake.

The question came rolling back as Ray rubbed sleep from his eyes: Why were we pulling out? And, if we were pulling out, what was the *Newport News* doing steaming, with urgency, toward Vietnam?

Chapter 3

Into Charlie's Face

The rigorous training continued as they steamed across the Pacific on May 2. By evening they had arrived at the Island of Guam, their last fuel stop before continuing on to Subic Bay, Philippines. They departed Guam at midnight and continued their journey. The weather remained warm and clear and they arrived at Subic at noon on May 6. The ship had made the 11,400-mile voyage from Norfolk to Subic Bay in twenty-two days and ten hours, her overall average speed working out to 23.2 knots. She had slowed to ten knots on one occasion to refuel from a tanker and lost additional time transiting the Panama Canal and stopping briefly at Pearl Harbor. For the sailors, there would be a forty-eight-hour stay in this last port of call before entering the war zone. Here, in this isolated Pacific Island harbor, other new experiences would unfold.

First priority for the majority of the crew was to seek some relaxation and enjoyment. Subic Bay in May of '72 was prepared to accommodate any and all of their needs. The Naval base was the largest support base in the world at the time, outside the United States. It had been growing with the escalation of the war since the 1960s and had peaked to a sprawling community of several hundred thousand service personnel. As it had grown, the indigenous culture surrounding it had thrived. Around the Naval base perimeter, a foray into Olongapo City offered everything from bars, night clubs, brothels, and gambling casinos to clothing shops, clip joints, hock shops, and sidewalk vendors selling "monkey on a stick," the name given to whatever form of meat was available to grill over charcoal fired grills fashioned from halved fifty-five gallon fuel drums.

Olongapo City, Subic Bay, Philippines

The Philippine people had not missed an opportunity to cash in on this macroeconomy; a continually rotating clientele of young Americans seeking refuge and rest from their long, and often mundane, periods at sea and in the air, doing their part to support Uncle Sam's efforts to stop the spread of Communism. Some of the men—the minority really—were combatants, while the greater portion were support personnel manning the hundreds of supply ships, ammunition ships, and tankers at sea off the coast of Vietnam. All of them though, combatants and support people alike, would return to this Philippine port after working long, hard, twelve-hour days at sea. Without having any release from the tensions, stress, and boredom accumulated after a month or more at sea, their four or five days of liberty were spent in terms of excess: excess drinking, excess drugs, and excess debauchery.

For "five dollar U.S." any man could buy himself the "services" of any of a large number of very attractive young women, mostly of Asian, Polynesian, Hispanic, or American-Asian heritage. A man could buy those services plus an overnight stay, hotel room included, for only $15. The nightclubs, whorehouses, and casinos remained open twenty-four hours every day, and every form of con game existed in the underground swill of humanity in this trashy waterfront city. From phony drug deals to frequent muggings, the name of the game was to separate the GIs from their hard-earned cash. The crew of *Newport News* had seen seedy ports of call in the past, but even the least attractive of these in South America and the Caribbean had been several levels above the depths of Olongapo City.

Forty-eight hours was not a lot of time to party, but this crew was heading to a war. Their future was uncertain, their tension was high, and their adrenaline was peaking, not to mention the pent-up testosterone associated with a long voyage at sea for a crew of 1,100 males whose average age was twenty. It was one last chance to partake of whatever pleasures could be wrested from this strange place.

It was also a time to reflect and tie-up loose ends, including phone calls to loved ones back in the states, updating one's will, and perhaps buying a tax-free gift at the Naval base exchange to ship home to a sweetheart. The hours flew by like seconds in this surreal place. Before they realized it, the ship and its crew were underway again. Upon clearing the harbor at Subic Bay, *Newport News* cranked up her boilers to full power and steamed at thirty knots to rendezvous with Task Unit 77.1.2 off the coast of Vietnam, arriving at 6:30 p.m., May 9.

Organizational command structures within the Navy were familiar among operations personnel. Their unique numeric identifiers were made up as required according to standards, and were activated and deactivated as needed to accommodate ever-changing conditions.

As with all things in the military, they followed a predetermined method based on contingency planning. A fleet commander would designate specific organizations from the vast resources at his disposal, and his staff and planners assigned designations to each part of that organization.

For example, The Pacific Fleet was known as the Seventh Fleet. The fleet was further broken down into Task Forces, Task Groups, Task Units, and Task Elements. Task Force 77 was the overall force charged with offensive naval activities against North Vietnam, while Task Force 70 was the overall force providing gunfire support to land forces in South Vietnam. Both of these Task Forces were made up of "assets" belonging to the Seventh Fleet. The number following the first decimal point indicated the Task Group (TG), in this case .1. This might indicate a surface warfare group. Next came the Task Unit (TU) designation, .2, indicating fast-attack gunfire strike. Each individual ship would then have its own Task Element (TE) number following the next decimal.

In this manner, as missions were defined each operational part of the fleet had its own identifier. Thus, the entire fleet could be mixed and matched and still have each segment easily identified. These identifiers would change often. It was a constantly changing game that referred to units, not by name, but instead by what might, to the enemy, seem like randomly chosen, otherwise meaningless numbers.

For example, a Task Unit is needed to perform an attack on a known target. Its mission planners decide they need three cruisers and two destroyers to make that attack, so they put a Task Unit together using fleet assets; designating them as the following Task Elements. First, they assign the TU a number such as 77.1.2, then they pick the elements necessary to perform that task and assign them more specific numbers. *Newport News* might be the central element of TU 77.1.2, and as such would be TE 77.1.2.1. The *Oklahoma City,* a slightly smaller cruiser would be TE 77.1.2.2, followed by the *Providence* designated TE 77.1.2.3, and then two destroyers designated TE 77.1.2.4 and 77.1.2.5.

Since joining Task Force 77, *Newport News'* Teletype traffic in the main communications center (Maincom) was continuous. Message traffic from everywhere was coming together to coordinate the ship's entry into a Task Group and then a Task Unit. This was a second reason for these cryptic identifiers; it made it hard for anyone listening in on our operations planning to discern what ships or elements were being discussed. The Navy was preparing the ship for something only a few of her crew would know about until the very moment was upon them.

Maincom was the name given to the Teletype Center that also included a message processing and routing center as well as a cryptography room. The sign on the door read, "SECURE AREA–AUTHORIZED PERSONNEL ONLY," and it was quite literal in its meaning. A four-digit cipher lock fixed permanently to the bulkhead near the heavily reinforced door made it clear this was a high security area. Inside, like most of the interior of the ship, this twenty-by-thirty-foot compartment was illuminated with soft fluorescent lighting, which made the light green walls ("bulkheads" in sailor talk) seem relatively soft in texture and hue. Highly polished, dark green asphalt tiles finished the floors, which all sailors came to refer to as decks. This color scheme was carried out throughout the ship, from the main deck down. There were times when it seemed quite boring in its uniformity, but the functionality of these surroundings had been a long established convention in Navy ship design. The purpose of the subdued illumination and soft colors would insure the sailors' workstation environment kept their eyesight adjusted to lower light levels and added a psychologically soothing affect. Windowless and with only one access door, Maincom was purposely isolated from other workspaces on the ship. What transpired within this secretive place was not for the general crew to know.

Because the room was air-conditioned, a constant hiss of moving air along with the constant din of electrical machines added to the auditory reality. Chattering teletype consoles, the whir of copy machines, and occasional cross-talk from the intercom system, (a system which connected the communications department to the bridge, combat information center, and various other operations stations, and was commonly referred to as the "squawk box") drifted in and out of the men's consciousness.

A second cipher-locked door led to the Off-line Crypto Room, an even more secretive space to which only a select few of the communications personnel had access. At present, the Crypto Center was inundated with top-secret message traffic.

Some sections of the comm center were cordoned off and manned by officers only. A new level of security classification was becoming known to many for the first time. At the top of selected messages the bold letters stood out: **Top Secret OEO** (officer's eyes only). Before anyone on the distant end of a teletype circuit communicating with the *Newport News* could send one of these special messages, he had to talk personally with a communications officer who was required to furnish his own personal identification code. It was also necessary for this officer to insure there were no other personnel near enough to see what was coming over the machine he was tending. Despite this, there were some of the message center people who, out of necessity, had to assist the comm officers with the processing of these messages. Dave was one of them. Dave and Ray had been good friends since radio school, had gotten their Top-Secret clearances at the same time, and, despite instructions to the contrary, occasionally shared information between each other, as did some of the other close buddies in the comm crew.

Ray's duty station was directly below Maincom in what was called Radio Central (a.k.a. Radio One). He and the four or five others who worked in communications engineering occupied three adjoining spaces known as Classified Control. When they were off duty, another team took their place to keep these operations running continually. These work areas were the nerve center of the ship's communications systems. Here, activity was at a peak; preparations were made, systems checked and double-checked, and contingencies reviewed to assure double and triple redundancy on all of the tactical command radio systems. It was evident that something big was afoot.

Ray knew from his training and experience over the past two and a half years that this kind of preparation was not routine. Crypto equipment Ray had never seen before had been installed between Guam and Subic. Its operation and use had not even been discussed until now. Since leaving Subic he and a few other radiomen had been trained in the use of the KY-14, a new FM voice radio scrambler that guaranteed secure communications within a tactical Task Force. These black boxes were the latest generation of electronic devices to protect against enemy monitoring of communications among U.S. military elements. Training for this equipment included how to destroy it if the ship was in danger of falling into enemy hands.

Ray, and several others who worked in this space, were the crypto clerks of the department. They were responsible for destroying all electronic cryptographic equipment along with any related documents and publications should the ship fall into the hands of the enemy. This had a sobering effect as Ray came to grips with its importance. The instructions and drills left no uncertain details. Ray was not to leave his station until all classified publications had been taken out of the crypto safe and jettisoned over the side in lead-weighted bags. Once this was accomplished, he was to return to the crypto equipment and assist in physically destroying it using fire axes and sledgehammers. The only way to leave his station otherwise was if the ship was sinking and the command to abandon ship had been given,

At 5:00 p.m. Ray, having been rescheduled for night duty on this watch rotation, strolled down the passageway to meet Dave. The taller, fair-haired figure leaning against the propped hatchway wrung his fingers nervously as Ray approached him. The two men walked together to the mess decks for dinner. One look at Dave told Ray that he knew something.

"You know something I don't Bumbstead," Ray said to his buddy as they made their way through the chow line.

Dave looked around and lowered his voice. "Wait 'til we sit down."

They chose a table isolated from the rest of the crew. Dave leaned forward and spoke quietly.

"We're going right into the tiger's mouth Ray, as far north into Vietnam as you can go, right near the Chinese border. I'm scared shitless man!"

"Where, Hanoi? Where are we going?"

"Haiphong."

"Where is Haiphong?"

"It's the biggest port city in Vietnam, about twenty miles east of Hanoi; it's where all the supplies and munitions come in to North Vietnam from Russia and China."

"Holy Shit!" Ray's eyes widened as he tried to keep his voice down. "Gung Ho, motherfucker, we're gonna go kick Charlie's ass."

"Screw that," Dave said, "there are Russian and Chinese ships there. It's the most heavily defended place in North Vietnam, and they have hundreds of 130 and 155mm cannons and missiles. Not only that, Seventh Fleet has been seeding the harbor with mines since last week."

"Yeah, but our guns shoot nearly twenty miles. We won't even see the place, we'll be over the horizon."

"No, that's just it, some of the targets are inland between Haiphong and Hanoi. We have to get within a couple of miles of the shore to hit them. Also, there is an intended psychological effect they're trying to achieve. They want to do it right in Charlie's face, up close and personal. It's nuts!"

"Dave, don't worry. Do you really think the U.S. Government is going to put a big heavy cruiser in a place where it could be sunk or disabled in enemy territory? There must be more to it than that. They must know something you don't."

"Listen to me! It's not just us either. COMSEVENTHFLT is going to be on the *Oklahoma City,* and the *USS Providence* and two destroyers, the *Buchanan* and *Hanson*, are going in as well."

Ray let the words sink in and thought for a few seconds before speaking again. "Calm down buddy, the Navy is not going to risk three thousand men in one operation! There must be other stuff here that you don't know about, it can't be that risky."

"I'm telling you Ray, I've been in the Off-line Crypto Room with Lieutenant Eisenhower for the last two days. I've seen all of it. They call it a strike plan. First, there are naval gunfire strikes, then the mines are supposed to be activated after we leave the harbor to barricade future shipping. The messages are all Top Secret OEO. I'm technically not even supposed to be there, but we don't have enough TS cleared officers with crypto training to handle all the message traffic. If Eisenhower knew I was telling you this I'd be in a world of shit, so you have to give me your word you won't say anything. I mean it."

"Hey, you know me. We have an agreement—nothing goes anywhere, but I think you're worrying too much."

"Maybe, but I know what I've seen, and it looks like craziness to me. I just had to tell somebody, I can't keep it to myself."

"Well what does Eisenhower say about it"?

"Shit, you know him, he wouldn't say shit if he had a mouth full of it."

"When is this going to happen?"

"I don't know. The specifics on times aren't being given, but if you've been paying attention to the navigation coordinates, we've been steaming due north since meeting up with the Task Group. I think we're going to loiter a safe distance off shore until the time is right."

"Son-of-a-bitch, we're really goin' in; we're gonna pounce right on their communist motherfucking asses. This is a good thing Dave, I'm psyched!"

"Yeah, you and everybody else that knows. Not me, I think it's scary as fucking hell, I'm freakin' out! What's with you all of a sudden Ray, I've never seen you act like this?"

"You may have forgotten Dave, but I sure as hell haven't forgotten about my nephew Brian and the thousands of other young American patriots who have been killed in this dip-shit war. It's about goddamned time somebody got off their ass and did something to these fuckers. And we're going to do it! Bring it on."

Chapter 4

Radio One

At 7:00 p.m., Ray made his way back to Radio One. He entered through the forward main deck hatch, descended one level past Maincom, and continued down the steel stairwell that snaked behind the heavy iron encasement of number two main battery turret. At the bottom of the stairs he opened the watertight door, stepped into his workspace, and secured the door again behind him.

Andy, known to his friends as "Bird," a shortened version of his surname, was sitting in the swivel chair at the operator's desk. Bird ran the fingers of his left hand through the locks of his bushy, sandy-colored hair, then drew them across his cheek contemplatively viewing the status board. With his other hand he gestured in the air with a grease pencil as though accounting for steps in a process. He ended with a nod of certainty and turned to acknowledge Ray.

"Raymond, you got the comm, Dude. Hope you have a good night, I hear it's going to be exciting."

"What have you heard Bird? Are we goin' into North Vietnam?"

"That's the buzz, heard it from the top. Commander Stroud and Chief Yerks will be in charge upstairs and down here, respectively. They want you to have Mike man the sound powered phones when we are at GQ; backup in case we lose power or take a hit somewhere. The Chief said he'd be down to go over details with you at about 9:00."

Ray strolled to the coffeepot and poured himself a cup as Bird continued. "So what have you heard about this strike shit?"

"If I told you, I'd have to kill you," Ray replied with a grin.

"Come on asshole, you know we have the same level of security clearance and nobody can take anything off this ship as long as we're at sea anyway. So what's the deal?"

"Who have you been talking to?" Ray asked.

"The Chief and Commander Stroud filled me in on some things. I know we're going into North Vietnam and we're going to make strikes on coastal defenses and military targets in the Haiphong area. Chief says we'll probably take counter battery (incoming artillery) from enemy shore installations. They say there hasn't been a gunfire raid of this size conducted since World War II."

"Well it sounds like you know more than I do at this point. I can't add anything to that, but I did hear the same stuff from another source."

"Yeah, me too. Cooper down in CIC talked to me a little earlier and said the ship is fully armed and ready to rock 'n' roll with all she's got. They're programming targets into the main battery fire control system and the five-inchers are on standby to take on any counter battery targets," Bird continued as he moved toward the doorway. "I'm gonna go take a break and relax a little if that's possible. I might stop down later to see what's new."

"All right buddy, talk to you later," Ray said as he watched Bird disappear through the hatch.

Ray looked toward the far end of the room and exchanged a nod of greetings with Mike, his immediate subordinate, who was seated at one of the operator's desks in the rear of Radio One. He was one and a half years younger than Ray and Bird, and one of the newer members of CR Division. Mike had an air of nervousness, like a skittish freshman in a frat house full of seniors. Mike's youthful features seemed exaggerated to Ray. As he observed, he could tell Mike was writing on what appeared to be letter stationery and pausing in thought between his efforts. Ray walked slowly toward Mike and sipped at his coffee.

Mike would be his backup person and would man the sound powered phones while the ship was at General Quarters. "GQ," as it was known, meant battle stations. General Quarters, "Condition Zebra," was the highest degree of readiness a naval ship could attain; it meant the eminent probability of enemy hostilities, "Battle Stations." In this case, the likelihood of counter battery was anticipated.

When readiness Condition Zebra was in effect, all watertight doors and hatches were closed and secured as tightly as possible. This was done by "dogging" the doors; turning the eight heavy, steel levers known as "dogs," and then applying torque to them with a dogging wrench. As torque was applied to each of the dogs, the door was forced tightly against a rubber seal that prevented leakage in the event the ship's watertight integrity was compromised. The circular "hatches" were secured by turning an iron wheel that worked four mechanically connected dogs to achieve the same result.

In this condition of readiness, each person, team, or watch crew, as well as those off duty in their berthing compartments, would be sealed into the space they occupied and would remain there until GQ was terminated or it became necessary to escape due to life threatening circumstances.

The sound powered phone circuit functioned without need of electrical power, thus making it impervious to power outages. These extra measures were employed each time a ship went into combat.

"Well Mike, you ready for this shit? Word is it's gonna happen tonight."

"Yeah, I've been hearing the same stuff. I hope everything comes out all right, it seems unreal to me." Mike had a personal connection to the Vietnam War as well; his sister's husband had been a Huey pilot and was shot down. Several of his crewmembers died, and he lost a leg. Now both men realized they were in the place where their respective relatives had fought and suffered.

Ray and Mike traded stories as they attended to their duties. For the most part, the day crew had made all the preparations. Ray and Mike reviewed all of the settings and rechecked the status boards, which displayed systems information on the hundreds of pieces of radio gear that made up voice circuits interconnected to various parts of the ship through the switchboards in Radio One.

Switchboards were what Radio One was all about. Approximately half of this area, the size of a motor home, was dedicated to three vertical banks of switching panels that extended from a foot above the floor to a height of about six feet. The outboard bulkhead of the room was lined with "operator's consoles," a row of four executive-sized desks. Each of these had a typewriter, a telegraph key, several speakers, and four radio receivers, each about the size of a microwave oven. To the right (or aft) of these consoles were additional banks of receivers.

On the facing wall were antenna tuning consoles, a crypto safe for classified publications, and a four-by-two-foot table with a fifty-five cup coffee pot and numerous incidentals. To the rear of this wall, a watertight door led to the radio Chief's office; a six-by-ten-foot space with a desk and filing cabinets. On the forward end of the inboard wall, farthest from the Chief's office, was the Radio Central Operator's desk, which had a telephone, intercom station, typewriter, several voice radio remotes, and two large Lucite status boards that graphically represented all radio equipment in use. Two feet to the left of this was the entryway into unclassified control, a space about twice the size of Radio One containing electronic cryptography and diagnostic equipment secured to steel shelves or "racks." Further inboard, straddling the centerline of the ship, was the On-line Crypto Room where the controllers, a team of about four or five, attended to the engineering end of the radio-teletype and crypto systems. There were no watertight doors or hatches separating Radio One, unclassified control, or the On-line Crypto Room, rather they had open doorways. The radio one and control staff passed back and forth as one watch team.

Occasionally, the controllers would call for a "posit," the ship's current navigational position, for use with communicating with the communications engineering people at NAVCOMSTA Subic in the Philippines. A capital ship like the *Newport News* had constant contact with at least one, and usually two, shore-based communications stations at all times. The teletype message traffic continued on these circuits twenty-four-seven; continually protected by electronic crypto equipment. For the ship to keep this constant "termination" running required frequent changes in radio frequency and modes of operation. The controllers orchestrated this function and relayed the ship's position to the COMSTA several times each day. With these exceptions, everything else in the communications department was quiet. The ships in TG 77.1.2 had been communicating with each other by semaphore and flashing light since early afternoon in an effort to maintain radio silence while approaching their objectives.

At 11:15 p.m. the voice of Captain Walter F. Zartman came over the public address system: "This is the captain speaking. In a little less than three hours we are going to do what hasn't been done by the U.S. Navy in nearly twenty-five years. We've come all this way to meet up with *USS Oklahoma City*, *USS Providence*, and the destroyers *USS Hanson* and *USS Buchanan* to make coordinated gunfire strikes against military targets in North Vietnam. Now I want you to know that this is not a drill, and it is not an easy mark. In all likelihood we will encounter enemy artillery and possibly surface craft or aircraft. But this is what we've been training for, and we are the best-trained crew in the Navy right now to carry out this mission. All you men have to do is do your part the way you've been trained and we'll all come through this in good shape. So I want to see every last one of you alert and sharp. I want to see all your peckers up!"

So it's official, Ray thought, as the captain's words hung in the silence that followed. *That's the real deal, no doubts about what's going down now. There it was, all laid out by the captain in an address to all hands.*

Mike and Ray talked with Chief Yerks and Commander Stroud several times in the next hour, making last minute checks and trying to anticipate ways to quickly and efficiently restore voice communications circuits among the Task Group, should they degrade. The focus was on maintaining the flow of information among the five ships as they undertook their mission. The ships would be maneuvering rapidly and might need to deviate from their courses instantly to counter enemy threats. This meant a higher likelihood that sensitive electronic systems could malfunction or lose synchronicity with one another. If the Task Group was moving rapidly through darkness with very little visual reference, it was especially reliant on good verbal communications. But since FM Secure Voice technology of the day was limited, it would not be unusual to have “blind spots,” or areas of blocked signal coverage as the ships changed positions relative to one another. To counter this it was necessary to have several co-phased antennas on each FM transceiver-set used for this purpose. This presented tuning problems and caused other anomalies like “signal splatter” and “transceiver detuning.” It was all fairly intricate and required constant monitoring and responsiveness to stay ahead of the game. Instantaneous switching of transmitters, receivers, and antennas to backup equipment or alternate equipment locations would be a real requirement. Close quarters communications exercises had shown this to be a weak point.

Chief Yerks was a little shorter than average height and a healthy-looking fifty-year-old who resembled Bing Crosby in a khaki uniform. He had a kind smile and fatherly eyes. The Chief took great care and spoke softly while instructing Ray and Mike as he moved from one equipment stack to another going over the important aspects of each. He was a technical wizard, having served nearly thirty years in the Navy and being one of those technicians who made it his goal to be continually aware of all aspects of telecommunications science. The Chief had backup systems configured in every possible way to insure the fast, reliable, and secure communications for which Navy communicators were revered.

There would be one primary frequency with which all of the ships would be tied together; these radio remotes would be strategically located throughout the ship. The bridge and combat information center, as well as fire control plotting, would be in contact with each other and the other ships in the flotilla at all times. At least that was the objective. There would also be a back up or secondary communications frequency should the enemy jam the primary.

The next line of defense was battery powered mobile units, though these were generally less reliable than the larger systems. Along with this tactical command circuit, there would be a link to tactical air units and reconnaissance aircraft positioned over the enemy area.

As Ray, Mike, and Chief Yerks talked about the details of these systems, it was beyond Ray's realm of reality that, simultaneously, an entirely different type of electronics technology was being used in the same place and the same time.

Ivan was one of Ray and Bird's best buddies outside of the Radio gang. "Doc," as he was known, was a rather slight, 5'7" and maybe 150 pounds. He had dark features, brown eyes, and a sparse black mustache. He looked fit, not a weakling by any means. His physique suggested wiry, rugged strength. Doc came from the Bad Lands of Montana, and Ray thought he might have Native American genealogy in his background, and perhaps some French blood as well. He spoke softly and with precision, which bespoke an obvious intelligence.

At this moment, Doc was squirreled away in a tiny, equipment-filled room in the superstructure of the ship. Aft of the bridge and forward of the ship's stack was an unobtrusive, barely noticeable domain, which few of the ship's crewmembers even knew about. The sign on the door simply said, "ECCM AUTHORIZED PERSONNEL ONLY."

"Electronic Counter Measures" was the term given to that segment of the defense electronics industry that had been engineered in the early years of World War II, the first radars and other types of electronic detection equipment. ECCM, which stood for Electronic Counter *Counter* Measures, was a further development that dealt with active deception or interference with the enemy's electronic communications and detection systems. The distinction was slight, and both terms were common and often used synonymously.

Doc was a specialist in this field. He had been trained for nearly three years in the operation of one particular piece of ECCM equipment, the SPS-29. This was a radar set with a number of very interesting capabilities. Doc was currently playing "music." Playing music was Doc's job. He was like a DJ, playing tunes out on the air to a select group of listeners; these listeners were the enemy. What the SPS-29 operator did was detect enemy radars, determine what they were, what each was used for (fire control, surface search, air search, etc.) and alter the radar returns so that the information showing up on the enemy's radar screen was erroneous.

Ray and Doc, and most of the others aboard *Newport News*, did not know that the other cruisers and aircraft in the region were playing similar tunes and had been for weeks. Operation Custom Tailor had been planned in great detail for months. The overall effect of this electronic warfare was that the North Vietnamese military regime in the Hanoi/Haiphong area knew that something would be happening in their area, but the kicker was, they had no idea when. This served three important functions. First, it was psychologically degrading to be bombarded by all the electronic interference. Second, it took the enemy's focus off their main thrust, the offensive into South Vietnam, and made them focus on defense. Third, the North Vietnamese had to continually test and calibrate their defensive electronic equipment, which gave the good guys the chance to monitor and define the locations and functions of those enemy systems.

There were also other variables in this electronics equation: SuppRad was another of those nondescript, seemingly innocuous areas in the superstructure of the Heavy Cruiser *Newport News*. Within this area, a space which Bird and Ray were familiar with because of an occasional need to support SuppRad's equipment needs, were three members of CR Division who, strangely, nobody knew very much about. They were communications technicians, CTs in naval jargon. But this was actually a misnomer, because these men were not just technicians in telecommunications technology—they were spooks. They gathered intelligence and actively deceived the enemy. All were fluent in numerous Asian dialects and proficient at mimicking and interfering with enemy intelligence efforts. It had vaguely occurred to Ray at some point that these three men, who stuck close together and rarely fraternized with the other communications people, were different. They wore no rate or rating badges on their uniforms; instead they wore simple olive drab fatigues without markings. Much later, Ray learned that they weren't actually Navy personnel, but were in fact employed by the CIA.

By design however, the complete picture, from where Ray or Doc or the rest of the crew stood, was impossible to perceive.

Chapter 5

Thunderstorm

Now the ship was quiet. Mike and Commander Stroud were seated, Mike at an operator's station with his headset and microphone plugged into the sound-powered intercom system, and the Commander in a chair near the Radio One operator's desk. Commander Stroud could not resist the urge to be in Radio One where he could hear the action and oversee the operations for which Ray and Mike were responsible. At the last minute he had switched assignments with Chief Yerks with the understanding that each could transit the two watertight doors and single flight of stairs between Maincom and Radio One as needed.

As the Communications Officer, Stroud was highly respected for his technical expertise. Stroud was a "Mustanger," which meant he had worked his way up through the enlisted grades as a radioman, then through the warrant officer program, and had received a commission as a Lieutenant the hard way. His expertise and training in all phases of communications made him a specialist of high caliber. Moreover, his background enabled him to communicate extremely well with his enlisted personnel and highest level officers simultaneously, a valuable asset in this sometimes-difficult culture. Just prior to departure from Norfolk, he had been promoted to the rank of Commander, the highest rank obtainable for an LDO (limited duty officer). His presence was always a comfort to his subordinates.

At present the Commander, dressed in neatly pressed khakis and sitting with his back to one of the operator's desks, was calmly sipping coffee from an oversized, cobalt blue mug. He paused and gazed thoughtfully into it for one second and then drew it near his nose, savoring the steamy aroma of the inky, black liquid. Emblazoned on the glossy ceramic was a bright white, lightning bolt logo and lettering that read, "COMSECONDFLT Communications; Fast, Reliable, Secure." The phrase reminded Ray of much milder duty.

Ray could not seem to get settled. Though his function was principally a passive one, which involved listening and being aware in order to make any adjustments necessary, adrenaline was beginning to flood his bloodstream. An observer of the scene in Radio One would have soon realized all three men were at a level of heightened awareness and well past the onset of the fight or flight response. In fact, this was true of most, if not all, of the men of Task Group 77.1.2

On the bridge of *Newport News* the combat watch detail was straining to see any sign of enemy action on the distant horizon. They were now in North Vietnamese territorial waters. The night was cool and dark, moonless. In the red hue of the battle lighting, their eyes had adjusted as the evening had advanced, and now their night vision was keen. The topside watch crew manned various locations about the many weather decks of the ship. The relative wind rushed by their ears with a hissing sound at a speed of thirty knots. The ocean was calm. Those with the best night vision had been singled out in the early stages of their careers to be part of the ten percent of the crew responsible for observing, assessing, and deciding what actions would be necessary. Captain Zartman was not alone among the people who held this distinction, but he was, by intent, one of the few people in the Navy who possessed the skills and training to be in command of this ship. The ship was moving fast. Even to the men in Radio One, three decks down, directly behind the number two main battery turret, that was clear.

A "turret," as opposed to a gun "mount," extends inside a steel "silo" or tube from the main deck all the way down to the keel at the bottom of the ship. Because it is incorporated into the structure of the ship, it can disburse the energy of recoil from the firing of its massive guns to structural members surrounding it. The encasements of the eight-inch guns of *Newport News'* main battery were approximately twenty-five feet in diameter and had armored walls eight inches thick. There were ammo-handling spaces distributed at various levels around these silos to provide speedy access and close proximity to the loading and replenishing required to fire at sustained high rates. A gun "mount," by contrast, is a smaller caliber, self-contained system that is fixed with a swivel base to the surface on which it is mounted. Turrets housed the larger, main battery guns, while the smaller secondary battery was made up of gun mounts.

Loading an eight-inch shell casing into turret three

Radio One, with its humming electronic equipment and banks of switching panels, was located one-third of the distance back from the bow of the ship, just behind the second of two forward turrets, and three decks below the forward-most five-inch mount. Right now, this section of the ship was alive with energy as "gunners mates" manned the weapons systems.

As was normal when the ship was traveling in a straight line, there was only a small sense of movement. When *Thunder*'s boilers were at a full head of steam, the ship rolled gently from side to side in response to the torque generated by her propellers. Added to this were mild up and down oscillations created by the nearly non-existent swells of the calm seas.

The voice radio networks, important to the operation of the Task Group, along with backup, emergency, and international distress circuits, emitted a collective background hum that seemed ominous. Occasionally, the faint sound of Morse code drifted through the mix. A burst of static periodically split the silence from distant stations working the same frequencies. Nearly thirty minutes earlier the ships had all gone to General Quarters.

The voice command network had come to life slowly; it had started with Radio checks. "Overwork this is Blackbeard, radio check, over."

"Blackbeard this is Thunder, read you loud and clear."

"Blackbeard this is Fighting Devil, read you loud and clear."

"Blackbeard this is Sharp Note, loud and clear."

"Blackbeard this is King City, loud and clear." As the individual Task "Element" Commanders checked communications with one another, Ray listened intently.

"Overwork this is Blackbeard, turn starboard three zero degrees on my mark. Ready, execute." The ships all began to maneuver. They were involved in a nautical ballet, choreographing the dance that would take the group into firing position. This would be a series of turns making the overall pattern one of zigzag configuration just in the off chance that one of Charlie's radars could see through all the junk that was being strewn into the radiological atmosphere. *This is the third hard turn*, Ray thought as the Task Group maneuvered in formation. He glanced over at Stroud who pursed his lips and stared intently at the deck under his feet, coffee cup in hand.

What the crew had felt as a hard list to the starboard side in the previous turn became suddenly neutral. For an instant, they were on an even keel but they then moved all the way over to a hard list to port. In reality, the angular shift as these turns were executed was probably only a mere ten degrees from vertical, but being inside a small closed room within this massive steel structure without any visual frame of reference made it seem like much more. The feeling was like being inside an elevator, but one that moved erratically, from side to side as well as up and down. *This is incredible*, Ray thought to himself. His mind's eye could see four other ships in close quarters, dancing their way up the slot with perfect synchronicity.

The ship seemed to be humming with energy. The sea sloshed loudly against her hull as she moved in brief spurts of motion that revealed sudden changes in direction to even the least experienced crewmembers.

Radio One was close to the centerline of the ship, about ten feet below the water line and surrounded by ammunition handling rooms and magazines. It was an accepted reality that Ray and the rest of these men spent their days and nights in a small, crowded room under water and flanked by thousands of pounds of explosives. This, however, was something of which they seldom spoke. Ray could hear the groaning of the steel members of the ship as its center of gravity was continually manipulated through long excursions of displacement; thousands of tons of steel framework was being thrown about like a speedboat on the surface of a lake. Occasionally, one could hear the clang and bang of ammo hoists and magazine machinery following the movement of the turrets as the ship moved around them. Electro-mechanical servos whirred and screeched as hydraulic cylinders manipulated the six huge barrels of the two forward turrets and shuttled the explosive shells through the main battery magazines. The guns were gyroscopically stabilized to remain trained on their targets as the ship moved about.

Amid all of these sounds, Ray's ears were tuned to the voices coming over the speakers he was monitoring. Mike listened to a different network with one ear covered by a partial headset. They were both hearing the weapons system sounds more rapidly and continually than in any previous training missions.

Mike's attention was on the backup intercommunications loop where all the ship's departments were tied together. This was an expansive, multi-party circuit, and the input arriving at Mike's ear was continuous. Topside watches were exchanging information with the bridge, and navigators were checking off visual landmarks. There were lights on the beach. "The gooks apparently don't have a clue we are here," Mike whispered.

To topside personnel it was a new experience as well. The three cruisers were barely discernible to one another in the dark night. With no lights showing, their haze gray color-schemes blended into the darkness. Only their bow waves and stern wakes stood out brightly against an otherwise black environment. The two destroyers skirted the flotilla. To the rear and outboard their wakes appeared to blend in, giving the impression that this could be a whole fleet of ships of enormous size, continuing behind for miles. For those near the eight-inch turrets, the decks and topsides seemed to be moving all around with the sea as the guns remained trained, as if frozen in time and space, on their dedicated targets.

No one spoke unnecessarily. Throughout the ship there were no human sounds except for the Task Group Commander's voice, and this only in the spaces involved with the ship's operation. "Overwork this is Blackbeard, final turn to firing leg, turn to port, six zero degrees in five, four, three, two, one, execute." The ships turned violently once more. There was dead silence, and then *Boom, Boom, Boom, Boom, Boom!*

Main battery firing off the coast of Vietnam

The main battery was firing at maximum rate, pumping out continuous nine shot salvos of artillery shells. In less than one minute, but what seemed to Ray like several, they halted, paused to acquire new targets, and resumed just as suddenly. Now the less alarming and much more erratic sound of the five-inch guns began from various locations on the ship. These were twin mounts, each firing at what seemed to be intermittent intervals. And then a third sound became apparent.

The first few were dull thuds that seemed far off, as if perhaps they were gun noise from the other ships. With increasing regularity they seemed to get closer and louder as the five-inch mounts continued to ramp up their rate of fire.

"They're firing at us," Mike said with concern, "we're taking counter battery from the beach." Ray looked at Mike whose eyes were wide and fixed as though he was in a trance. Mike was trying to focus his attention on the voices. Now there was cross-talk from several locations. Excited topside watches were spewing expletives and exchanging war-whoops and expressions of surprise. The background sounds of exploding shells and gun bursts further complicated the mix. Mike's eyes widened as he listened intently.

The Task Group command circuit was quiet for a moment then, suddenly, Blackbeard burst into presence again. "Overwork this is Blackbeard, turn port three zero degrees on my mark. Ready, execute!" The dance began again, but now the situation had changed. The ships were turning away. The dull thuds had become louder and more frequent, and the secondary batteries were firing sporadically as spotters called out relative bearings to muzzle flashes on the shoreline. The ship was listing first to starboard then to port and again to starboard, back and forth as the gun mounts whirred and creaked and boomed, firing now and again from all six of the secondary battery positions.

Suddenly there was a burst of three-inch fifty fire. No sooner had it started than someone yelled, "Cease fire on mount thirty-two," and the mount ceased fire as abruptly as it had began. The men would later learn that the overly excited three-inch mount crew had inadvertently opened fire on one of the destroyers, a case of mistaken identity. Thankfully, no hits were made.

Ray's pulse was racing. Though everyone seemed composed, for the next two minutes it seemed like everything stood still and, at the same time, moved wildly and chaotically around them. The room rose and fell and leaned alternately from side to side like an elevator in a tall building progressing up and down as the building swayed violently in an earthquake.

Gradually, and without their awareness, the muffled sounds became fewer and less intrusive and the shells fell farther away as the TG withdrew from its firing position. Topside, the lights of the harbor dimmed and then blacked out completely. It had taken only five or six minutes to complete the firing leg, but it seemed like an eternity to the crew.

The fact that the North Vietnamese could not react fast enough to black out their lighting systems meant they *had* been caught off guard. The shore batteries had responded, but the delay and inaccuracy of their fire proved they had been shooting manually at muzzle flashes. Their radars had been rendered ineffective. Since the ships were several miles away from them, moving at a relatively high rate of speed, the chances of the North Vietnamese gunners being able to pinpoint and zero in on what they could only see as a massive, distant fireworks display were quite slim. Much like bombers flying through flack-filled skies, the ships slid away from the action. Twenty minutes later the flotilla was again over the horizon from the perspective of the inhabitants of Haiphong. The TG stopped sailing the zigzag pattern and spread out into a less tightly packed formation rapidly making progress toward the Southeast.

In another twenty minutes the ships were safely beyond the enemy's range. No surface craft or airplanes appeared to be chasing them. They secured from battle stations and crewmembers began opening the watertight doors and hatches that had been sealed. Fresh air rushed in to the interior of the ship and everyone breathed more easily. Once again the captain's voice came to life through the speakers of the 1MC:

"This is the captain speaking. I want to congratulate everyone on a magnificent job. This was the first real action most of you have ever seen, and it came off exactly as planned. We fired seventy-seven rounds of eight-inch at two primary targets, and from all accounts, received about one hundred rounds of enemy fire from the coastal defense sites on the beach. Most of these went wide, although we did mark a number of near misses. It's evident from the night's action that the Vietnamese gunners were shooting at our muzzle flashes and had no way of correcting their aim to be truly effective at hitting us. The five-inch mounts fired another forty or so rounds and did an outstanding job of retaliating once the 130s opened up on us, and, in fact, we're quite sure we silenced at least a couple of them. Collectively, the Task Group put out an amazing amount of ordinance in a very brief period, and we observed several secondary explosions on the beach indicating that we probably hit our primary targets, which were munitions and fuel storage bunkers. By all indications there will be a good number of operations like this in the coming weeks. Let's all keep doing the same things and make this effort the very best we can. Keep your peckers up!"

Chapter 6

The Big Picture

The rest of the night was more routine. The ships broke formation, and each took up its individual logistics plan around dawn. It was still not discernible to the crew of the "big heavy," a name used by some to refer to *Newport News,* that the scheme of things was much more expansive than anyone imagined. The five ships had all been routed toward the area known as Yankee Station, a fleet support realm two hundred miles east of the Vietnam coast.

Nearly all of the crew had been awake for the greater portion of the night. The half that was off-duty during the midnight action had been unable to sleep. Without any information except the captain's addresses and the division monitor manning the sound powered phones in each berthing compartment, these 550 souls had been sequestered in their respective sleeping quarters during the action. To them the whole thing had been a whirlwind of confusion. The intuitive knowledge that the ship was maneuvering rapidly and unpredictably became entwined with sensations of sound and vibration as twenty plus guns of the cruiser fired with uncommon urgency. Bird, Jeffery, and the fifteen or so other members of CR Division had only been able to glean the most basic of facts from Kent, who had been the intercom operator. But, without question, they had been brought to the same level of excitement during the action. After it was over, the entire ship's crew was awake and charged with energy. As the crew exited their battle stations there was a surge of activity emerging into the passageways and spilling out onto the weather decks. The men were alive with conversation and expression.

By now, in the early morning light, there was nothing to see of the other ships. The earliest of those topside had caught the last flashing light sequences coming from the other members of the flotilla as the ships broke formation and headed each in its own way. Most of the crew was incapable of reading Morse code at the rate messages were sent, and even Ray and Bird who were trained in code had trouble making out the rapid light bursts of dots and dashes. They stood on the main deck at the starboard-side, forward watertight door behind turret two. They both needed a breath of fresh air. Mike had taken over the watch responsibilities in Radio One where, at this time, there was very little happening. Bird strained to see what was visible in the approaching eastern light as he spoke to Ray.

"Shit man, what the hell was happening through all of that? Fill me in on the details dude, it seemed pretty intense. Were there surface craft coming at us? What happened?"

"No, I don't think there were any targets moving at us, but the 130s and 155s were peppering the whole TG with artillery. The word is we took about two hundred rounds of CB throughout the flotilla, and about half of those were close enough to cause concern; that's according to the SITREP, situation report, the captain sent out a little while ago. Dave has been working on some TTY messages to CincPac. I guess they're really intent on assessing the action as quickly as possible. Speculation is this was the opener for a whole shitload of this stuff."

"No shit! I don't believe it; this is amazing. What was it like in One when it went down, could you hear what was going on?"

"Yeah, everything went really well from the standpoint of communications. There were no outages, everybody heard each other loud and clear, and the KY-14s performed perfectly. I didn't have to do anything but listen."

"So what was it like?"

"Well, mostly it was just the Task Group Commander giving maneuvering instructions to everyone. No wasted words, strictly business. We could hear short bursts of details on the secondaries a couple of times; they were apparently using them for inter-ship target coordination. Mike was relaying the stuff from the SPP circuit. There was a lot of information coming in, it was kind of unreal and hard to keep up with; everything was happening so fast, sort of like sensory overload in fast bursts."

There was a sense of anti-climactic emotion among the whole crew in the morning hours of May 10; all the preparation along with the acceleration of activity had brought them to an apex of energy that had been building over the last twenty-five days. Suddenly there had been a brief burst of intense action, and then, immediately after, it had fallen off to routine again, right as the men were pumped to the peak of their awareness. Those like Bird, and the rest of the off-duty personnel, never got back to a state of relaxation before they were again called upon to report to their watch stations.

The night crew as well was unable to relax until early in the afternoon. By this time, the ship was out to sea at a rendezvous point taking on fuel from the *USS Guadeloupe*. The men enjoyed the sunshine and blue water while taking pictures and observing the refueling. There were still short spurts of talk about the preceding night's action among friends, but by this time all topics had been covered and revisited nearly as much as anyone had patience for. The now off-duty crew grew tired, and by mid-afternoon most of them were again in their racks falling off into a warm comfortable sleep.

Ray was awakened at 6:15 p.m. after only three hours of sleep. With forty-five minutes to shower, shave, eat dinner/breakfast, and relieve Bird in Radio One, it was his second "hit the ground running" experience in the past twenty-four hours. The first conscious thought in his groggy mind was the seemingly immediate recollection that the ship and crew had just completed their very first foray into combat and that the experience, even though they had trained extensively, was totally foreign and unexpectedly frightening. The events of the previous night ran through his mind as he prepared to go back on duty.

After strolling the main deck while enjoying his after-dinner smoke, Ray stepped into Radio One and found Bird, face down on the operator's desk, asleep. Mike was sipping a cup of coffee and had already relieved Don, his watch counterpart. The three exchanged greetings. Bird slowly sat up and rubbed his eyes.

"Man, I'm beat," said Bird. "Everything is copacetic, nothing to update you on other than some interesting message traffic from Maincom."

"What's that?" Ray asked.

"Well, the big news is there was a major casualty report that went out today which wasn't acknowledged previously. It seems yesterday, around 6:30 p.m., there was a helicopter crash, which killed the Task Group Commander, his Chief of Staff, and his Operations Officer—the guys that were supposed to be in charge of the strikes last night."

"What!" Ray's amazement was apparent, "What are you saying? How can that be?"

"Hey, I'm just passing it on. Supposedly there's no question about it—Rear Admiral Robinson was killed along with his top two operations people, just a few hours before the raid on Haiphong. He was supposed to be the guy in charge; he had done all the planning and training for the operation."

"How the hell were they able to pull it off like that without the Admiral?"

"They had it all planned and detailed. COMSEVENTHFLT said 'go' and we went."

"Holy shit! That is amazing, they didn't even hesitate, didn't even . . . didn't even blink!"

"Hey, we're at war. Somebody gets it, you keep on going. I guess they didn't want anybody to know beforehand, because of the psychological effect; knowing the TG Commander was not with us would be a demoralizing factor, so they just kept it going as planned. COMSEVENTHFLT actually took control. He had all the information and details anyway. I guess it's designed that way for contingency purposes. Isn't that incredible?"

"Jesus, I guess it is." Ray let his mind absorb these facts as he drew his ritual cup of "watch coffee," having noticed the coffeepot's red light was on. While he followed Bird's conversation he stirred in his usual two teaspoons of powdered creamer and one of sugar.

Bird was a good friend and as considerate and efficient as anyone in the CR Division. Ray always knew that assuming the watch from Bird was a done deal. The two sailors equally prided themselves on being in full control and having intimate knowledge of their specialty and realm of responsibility. Having a freshly brewed pot of coffee upon starting the watch was as much a part of that as being totally aware of the condition and status of each piece of radio and crypto equipment in their inventory. It had been impressed on all of the men in this specialty that fast and reliable communications were as great a part of naval warfare as anything else in the equation—the equation which separated the winners from those who fell prey to them. They took their work seriously, and now were beginning to understand just how seriously it might affect their lives.

"Oh, I just remembered," Bird said, "Chief Yerks brought this list of frequencies down from Maincom a little while ago. He said it might give us another source of information while we're up north tonight. These are local AM radio freqs for the Haiphong/Hanoi area. These are supposed to be English speaking broadcasts from various places, some of which might be largely propaganda, but interesting nonetheless. I think he got them from SuppRad, do you know anything about those guys?"

"Ah, no, not really," Ray said. For the first time it occurred to him that it might be important to learn what SuppRad was all about. Until now he had only a vague notion that there was a place called

Supplemental Radio where some of the comm gang worked, but he did not know much more than that.

"OK, I'll get Mike on a couple of the 390s to scan them all and patch what he can find into a collective remote. We can keep a constant monitor on a few of them. Let's see, we've got eight or ten receivers to work with. So we're going back up north tonight? Same thing as last night? Back to Haiphong?"

"Actually, I think it's going to be south of Haiphong. There was a press release out today that announced the fact that Haiphong Harbor has been mined, and all shipping is barricaded. Nothing can get in or out of there, so I guess we aren't going there for a while. Targets are supposed to be some SAM sites and costal defense batteries as well as staging yards and other military targets on the Do Son Peninsula. They must've had this thing all drawn up and planned for months. Rich says there is a constant flow of strike plan messages coming in via teletype now."

"No kidding, it's amazing the way this has been kept hush-hush for all this time."

As Ray spoke, it dawned on him that the cross-talk and rumormill in CR Division itself was suddenly opening up to a new dimension. Of course, it was logical since the ship and its crew were now isolated from the outside world except for the contact they had through radio communications. There was a mutual feeling developing in the department that created a false sense of security. The people with high-level clearances did not feel quite as threatened about the urgency to keep things strictly on a need to know basis. Bolstered by the reality that they were all in this together and that whatever occurred onboard was a collective experience, the desire to share information outweighed the strict rule that details of communications were never discussed. A feeling prevailed that it was OK to share real information about their circumstances with those whose lives were at stake. At this point it had not gone beyond CR Division personnel, but already there were discussions that circumvented security level policies. Among them, junior enlisted personnel and those who held no security clearance at all had been accepted into this close circle of secrecy.

Bird bid his buddies good evening, expressing an urgent need to get horizontal and sleep off some of the grogginess that had overcome him. He had been awake and agitated at some level ever since the previous morning. For the majority of the crew it felt very much like jet lag. Their physiological clocks had been scrambled by the events of the past twenty-four hours.

Doc felt the need to talk with someone. He had gotten some information and details from the other electronics technicians, but only bits and pieces. The ETs were another secretive society among the crew. There were twenty or so of them on board, many of who held high level security clearances, but very few of them had real access to information of an exact nature. What they could glean from the radio and radar people was much less specific. Tooth worked on fire control radars, Doc had the SPS 29, and Herc was a crypto tech. The people they were most familiar with were all tied together in various elements of the operations department.

Doc dialed the three-digit number for Radio One. Ray picked up the phone and answered as prescribed, "Radio One, how may I help you, Sir?"

"Don't call me Sir, sailor, I work for a living," Doc retorted with a chuckle. "What the fuck are you up to Raymond?"

"Hey, Doc, how are you doing?"

Doc was a bright spot for Ray in an otherwise drab social atmosphere aboard the ship. They had been friends since early in Ray's time aboard the *Newport News*. Doc, some of his ET buddies, and a few of the radiomen from previous times had shared an apartment near Old Dominion University in Norfolk.

Ray, Bird, and Doc had spent time together going back a couple of years now. On the ship, the ECCM space, where Doc worked, had become one of the places they hung out together in off-duty moments. The three of them had set up a rather extensive stereo system which, despite the lack of speakers, had a network of high quality headphones with which they could all share their common interest in current music.

"Well, I was wondering if we could get together for a smoke break on the main deck sometime tonight. I don't think we're going to GQ for a while yet, what do you think?"

"I think that can be arranged," Ray answered, "I just need to check with my Chief to make sure he doesn't have anything scheduled. Let me call you right back."

They hung up and Ray dialed the Maincom number and asked for Chief Yerks. The Chief came to the phone and said he would be down to brief Ray and Mike at 9:00 p.m.. Ray acknowledged the info and asked permission to take a break for half an hour. The Chief gave him his blessing and hung up without further comment. Ray excused himself, telling Mike he was going topside for a breath of air. Mike nodded his understanding without leaving the bank of receivers he was busily manipulating. The penciled list of frequencies was sitting on the desk before him.

Doc and Ray met at the after-main deck hatch and stepped from the superstructure into the dusk of yet another warm and docile evening. There was no coastline to be seen, but there were two ships to starboard, perhaps 1,000 yards off. Flashing lights gave their initial location, and upon closer observation, Ray could see that the nearer of them looked like a cruiser. *Probably the* Oklahoma City, he thought.

"Looks like we're in for another night of excitement, Doc."

"Yep, the scuttlebutt is that we're going in again like last night," Doc replied. "Hey buddy, what can you tell me that I don't already know? I've just been getting a smattering of stuff from CIC and some of the bridge ETs that have been working the radar and crypto equipment. Heard we lost a couple of major officer types before the raid last night. What gives?"

"From what I've heard they were suiting up to do the Task Force command thing when the helo they were riding in crashed while landing on *USS Providence*. Never heard a thing until today and the TG never missed a beat, they put together another team and proceeded as planned."

"Man that's cold, seems like they would have taken time out to regroup or something."

"I guess this whole strike group thing has been planned for some time. They were actually waiting for us to get here before starting; they wanted the rapid fire eight-inchers to be with them."

Doc let the words settle in his mind and took a drag on his cigarette. "This sounds like pretty serious shit, I don't remember signing up for this stuff. These guys are a bunch of wild men, what the fuck is going on?"

"I think we're cranking up the war. As far as I know this hasn't happened before. There was a message that went to the press services today that said the U.S. has barricaded North Vietnam from shipping anything in or out. It looks like we're going to be ramping up the pressure from the sea. Also, the carriers are flying sorties around the clock; supposedly they've opened up areas that were previously off limits for bombardment. What was happening in ECCM last night?"

"Hell, I was running back and forth like a maniac. They had me flipping and switching different modes of operation; one minute we were throwing out garbage to clutter the air waves, the next we were zeroing in on their fire control and throwing in Doppler shifts to put our signatures all over the place—it was intense. We picked up a lot of lit-up gun radars trying to seek and lock on us. Sometimes there were three or four at once. CIC said the *USS Hanson* had a search from what looked like a Russian surface-to-surface missile radar. A couple of times I thought they had our number. Some of those counter battery rounds came close; I could hear shrapnel and water splashes hitting the bulkheads all the way up in my ECCM space."

"Yeah, we were getting the chatter on the SPP, some of those guys were pretty excited. So what is this, how many times can we repeat that stuff and get away clean?"

Doc peered through bifocals with thick black frames. Like many others of the crew, he appeared slightly disheveled and had a heavy four o'clock shadow. He looked at Ray for a second or two before replying.

"I don't know what you know about ECCM, but we can screw them up pretty damn effectively in the electronics realm. The SPS 29 can intercept known signal types. There are about eight or ten Russian radars that we are intimately familiar with. I don't know where the info comes from, but our equipment is designed to identify and deceive their equipment. We can make it look like a squadron of ships is several miles away from its real position. We can make one ship look like a flotilla of five, or five look like one big target two miles away from its actual position. We can also scatter their whole radar spectrum with garbage that makes their screen look white with little blips here and there, all around. They can't tell which blips are us and which are garbage."

"No shit! We can actually do that?"

"We can, and we are. That's my job when we go in, operate the twenty-nine. But the guys in CIC are calling the moves, I just run the equipment. Plus the other ships have an array of ECCM gear that works in concert and uses different tricks. I hear from Hercules that the spooks in SuppRad are playing all kinds of games too; supposedly they get on the VC comm frequencies and intercept and interfere with their command and control efforts. Charlie gets all screwed up trying to figure out what's going on."

"Christ Doc, this is pretty heavy shit. You probably know that the voice crypto equipment we're using on our command and control freqs is virtually unjamable. Those things put out a burst of static and then a squeal that sounds like noise. On the air, you can't tell if it's a radar or what. Meanwhile, on the operator's side of the circuit, they have perfectly quiet, loud, and clear comms. It's really neat stuff."

"Yeah, from what I see, we go in with impunity, march right up to their noses, and blow them away. They can't get a bead on us and have very little visual reference except when we fire."

"They still haven't figured out how to hide a muzzle flash have they?"

"No, and that's what the gooks are aiming at. They see our flashes when we open up, then they saturate the area with artillery, it's all they have."

"Jesus, I still can't believe this is really happening Doc. This is the furthest thing in my mind from what I expected to find in Vietnam, I thought the fighting was all in rice patties and jungles among grunts—that's the only thing we've ever seen in the news."

"Right, that and ground support air campaigns. Granted, the Navy and Air Force have been conducting those raids on enemy positions, but this is a new phase in my opinion."

"Well, it's either that or we haven't been hearing a whole lot about the secretive part of this war. That's a pretty likely possibility too."

These were all thoughts to consider, but as they made their way back to their stations, both Ray and Doc found themselves thinking they were imagining a far greater scenario than what was probably real. *I'm exaggerating this*, Ray thought to himself as he entered Radio One. By this time, Mike had finished tuning the R-390 receivers to the frequencies for the broadcast radio stations. Chief Yerks was filling Mike in on yet another technical aspect of radio communications as Mike listened intently. The Chief was that way. He considered training to be a constant process. Each time a particular mode, method, or function of a piece of equipment or a system was required, he took it upon himself to review the technical manuals and draw from his experience to insure that everyone was on the same page from the perspective of comm engineering and the capabilities and limitations of the equipment and systems.

The din of circuit monitors now was greater than the night before by about double. Ray's eyes met those of the Chief as he turned right and started toward the coffee pot once more. "What's it like up there Ray?" the Chief asked.

"Oh it's comfortable, dark, and quiet. We're doing about twenty knots probably, looks like the *OK City* is off the rear quarter to starboard. Can't tell who else is out there."

"There are at least five, counting us. They just made radio checks about ten minutes ago. Couldn't tell if it was all the same ships as last night or not," Mike offered. "Do you remember the call-sign Sharp Note?"

“I think so, but I only heard them once, everything else was strictly Blackbeard. They used a minimum of communications, pretty smart and intentional I’m sure,” said Ray.

“Exactly!” the Chief replied with enthusiasm. “That’s what I was just talking to Mike about. Even though these guys know they’re on secure voice radio, the culture of the way they communicate is designed, over long years of experience, so that even if the enemy was able to decrypt, which might be a possibility in some time and place, they still couldn’t tell much about what we’re saying. There’s a bare minimum of verbiage, only the necessary details. It’s a science in itself really.”

Chapter 7

Marks of War

The ships were coming to full power again—it was earlier this time, having gone to General Quarters at about 9:45 in the evening.

In Radio One, the radio frequencies had been cycled so that the primary channel for this night was a different one from that of the first raid. This would help to insure that any possibility that the enemy had determined what the comm channel was the night before would be thwarted. It was like a rather intricate shell game, and the variables in the technological portion of defense strategies were becoming more apparent to Ray. Not that the Navy had failed to include such concepts in the training of its personnel, but the intimate details were kept from the conscious knowledge of subordinates in a purposeful manner. Details were simply left in the category of "need to know," which was so readily cultured in these ranks of communicators.

Mike was now seated at the operator's chair twirling a pencil in the fingers of his right hand. Chief Yerks and Ray stood at the row of operator's consoles that lined the outboard wall of Radio One. The Chief was adjusting a receiver to hear one of the AM radio stations more clearly. It was broadcasting in broken English and muttering something regarding the treacherous endeavors of the Seventh Fleet war criminals that had unmercifully attacked Haiphong the previous night. The station, however, kept fading in and out and became obliterated at times with "radio spectrum jamming," which was being spewed from numerous resources in the area. There was an increase of Morse code traffic for that very reason; much of the commercial shipping world used Morse extensively. There were also many amateur operators communicating in this mode. CW (continuous wave) telegraphy was a strong mode of operation and was capable of maintaining or establishing communications when more complex modes were not adequate because of frequency clutter (jamming) or atmospheric anomalies.

The Chief had shown Ray and Mike a way to connect the audio from the sound powered phone circuit to a vox unit (operator's monitor); this enabled them to free one person from being the dedicated SPP operator. Now all they had to do was listen, hands free, and respond, if necessary, to any communications directed to them through the ship's backup intercom system. The atmosphere in Radio One was slightly more challenging in terms of keeping up with everything. For now, things were relatively quiet, but it wouldn't last for long.

"Overwork this is Blackbeard, turn to port heading three zero zero on my mark. Ready, execute." The dance began once more as everyone in the crew recognized the sharp, immediate turn and the listing of the ship. Again their mental state started to ramp up, and their pulse and breath rate began to climb. A few minutes later the speaker came to life again: "Overwork this is Blackbeard, turn port three zero degrees on my mark. Ready, execute." The ballet was progressing—a turn to starboard, another to port, then back again. The legs of the journey became shorter as they fell into a zigzag rhythm that headed in a westerly direction. The topside watches began to call out bearings to lights and other landmarks. There was a suspected muzzle flash that seemed to fall into doubt nearly as quickly as reported. A critical aid-to-navigation, which should have been located by now, was not observable, but the navigation team backed up their plots with other identifiable waypoints. The initial target acquisition coordinates were verified, the gun control computers were engaged, and the minutes ticked by as the Task Group approached its destination, a theoretical point calculated as close as possible with the technology available. Like a bomber under the control of its bombardier, the ship and its sisters were dedicated to the precision of a carefully planned mathematical equation that held, as its focal point, a set of coordinates calculated with corrections for speed and time that would make them arrive at a specific point where they would then unleash their fury.

These details were not readily accessible to Ray, nor were they to most of the men aboard the five ships steaming into harm's way. But nonetheless, they were predetermined and carefully planned by members of the military elite, three of whom had perished only hours earlier. What did occur to Ray was a true reality in the military realm—this was war. It was real; it was here and now, and nothing was certain except that there was a force out there known as "the enemy" who had no choice but to try, with all of its resources, to stop what was about to happen. *It doesn't get any more real than this*, he found himself thinking, *this is literally survival mode—it's them or us, and one or the other will lose. In that loss will be death and destruction, chaos and pandemonium, finality.*

He was beginning to realize his side had the upper hand. Technologically, the U.S. was much more advanced than the Vietnamese, and several steps above the Russian and Chinese suppliers of their war machine; just how far above and how much more superior was a question mark, but in the last thirty or so days it had become increasingly apparent that he was on the side that possessed superiority. This was a comforting thought.

Ray was ready, the Chief and Mike were ready, the crew was ready, Task Group 77.1.2 was ready, and they were all willing and able.

Just as it had the previous night, it came without notice. Twenty seconds into the firing leg, the guns erupted with max-rate salvos. This time, Ray noticed brief interruptions as the guns whirled electromechanically to their new positions. The second time through this scenario gave the men an edge they had not been able to perceive the first time. They were more aware of the background noises and conversations that permeated the TG communications links. The sounds of muzzle blasts from the other ships could be heard over the lookout network, and dull thuds from outgoing salvos of six- and five-inch artillery could be heard despite the muffling effect of the sea. The crackle of static as *Thunder*'s main battery unleashed its deadly projectiles made Ray realize that there were momentary outages related to the concussion absorbed by the ship when the guns fired. These were fleeting milliseconds at most, and not sufficient to knock the crypto gear out of synchronization, but he noticed them. If the situation worsened, it could mean a critical loss of communications among the Task Group. Ray reviewed the status board, going over the remote locations and equipment positions, while thinking through the process of making an immediate systems switch if needed. It was serious business, but he was confident he could respond.

The five-inchers began to fire sporadically now, and the first of the incoming rounds could be heard bursting in the air over the lookout monitor seconds later. "Shit!" one voice exclaimed topside. "Jesus," another yelled. "That's goddamned close!"

Ray pictured brilliant flashes of light—the muzzle flashes of nine eight-inch guns which the crew had seen only seldom, and never at night.

To those on deck, it seemed like the entire sky lit up as the outgoing salvos continued. The military called it "flashless powder," but was immediately intent on defining its terms. "Flashless meant flash *less*," and that was as good as it got. It was impossible to propel a

260-pound projectile without making a lot of noise and fire in the process. Topside, the crescendo peaked, and the noise and flashes grew more and more numerous as all five ships fired. Now there was the added chaos of intermittent incoming rounds that burst with ferocity among the flotilla.

It was as if two gigantic weather systems were fighting for control of a single parcel of real estate. The lightning and thunder grew blinding and deafening. On the beach, fires, explosions, bursts of artillery flashes, and plumes of illuminated smoke could be seen by those with binoculars. Off shore, from the perspective of the enemy on the beach, another huge thunderhead was raging. Not more than five miles apart, these two furies aimed all of their force at one another. To slug it out with artillery over open water at this close proximity was analogous to a duel between two gunslingers wielding forty-four magnums inside a darkened bedroom closet.

Ray recalled his conversation with Dave two days before—"military show of force," "demonstrated resolve." Ray's reality had changed, was still changing, and was very much undefined. The emotional component was hard to pinpoint; mostly it was about revenge. Brian was worthy of this, he was certain. *Take that you gook motherfuckers*, he thought to himself. *Die bastards, die!*

Chief Yerks responded before Ray realized he had actually spoken aloud. "What's that Ray? Did you say something?"

"Oh, I said let the motherfuckers die, Chief. The bastards deserve it."

"Gung Ho son, I don't disagree, they've had it coming."

Twice more that night the ships withdrew and sprang back upon coastal targets south of Haiphong. By 3:30 a.m. the guns fell silent, and the Task Group split into its five individual components once again. More information, more activity, and another address from the captain made clear that there would be many nights like this in the coming months.

Ray stepped out of the after-main deck hatch, leaving the mess deck after a hastily prepared ration of "mid-rats." Normally this occurred at midnight, but this night it had to wait until the Task Group secured from GQ. *Powdered eggs and spam*, he thought to himself. *That sucked.* As he turned downwind to light his cigarette he recognized Doc. Doc seemed preoccupied with something he was manipulating in his right hand.

"Yo, Doc, what are you doing?"

"Ray, come here and look at this." He stretched his arm in Ray's direction.

"What is it Doc?" Ray strained to see three yards away in the dawn shadows.

"It's incoming artillery shrapnel man! I found it between here and ECCM, well actually down here on the main deck, check it out."

As they looked at it, a passing gunners mate said, "Yeah, go up by T-One. There was a shitload of it up there, scratched the paint on the starboard side of the turret silo on T-Two and gouged some of the teak planking on the main deck, pretty amazing." After the gunners mate passed, Doc said, "Ray, I've been thinking about the odds. If we keep taking counter battery, the odds are they'll hit us at some point. What does that mean? OK, we're armored at the waterline from turret one all the way back to number three, which is about sixty percent of her length. The magazines and turrets are armored above as well, the superstructure is vulnerable to air bursts, a direct hit would cream topside personnel and those housed in the superstructure. That's me man! But I'm just one little guy in one little room. What are the chances?"

The two sailors walked forward and noticed a small group of men standing by the number one forward eight-inch gun turret in the distance. As they passed the starboard side forward five-inch mount they saw two sailors using fire axes to punch holes in spent five-inch shell casings. As each casing was tossed over the side, it splashed, filled quickly with water, and sank. Ray and Doc peered over the lifelines to see them disappear in the dark blue water.

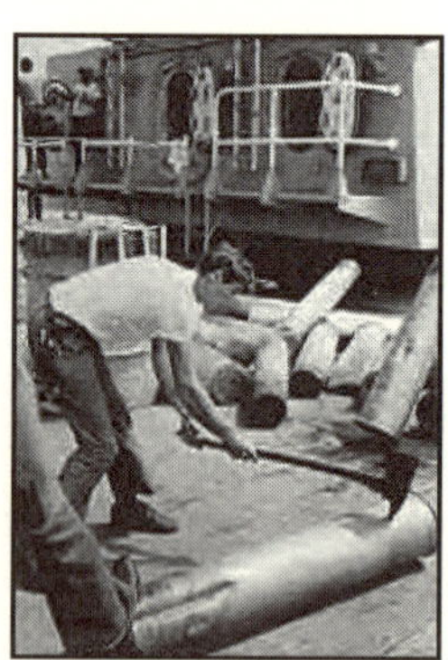

Axing shell casings

"Damn," Ray said, "look at all that nice brass going into the sea, there's got to be some money there don't you think Doc?"

"Hell, there must be twenty pounds of brass in each of those casings. That would be worth something in a salvage yard I would think."

Further forward, they both recognized the blue "NN" cap and gold filigree on Captain Zartman's head as the captain strode toward them. They snapped to attention, saluting smartly. The captain returned their salute and said, "At ease men, how are you guys doing this morning?"

"Squared away, Sir." Ray felt a nervous twinge as the words slipped from his lips. *That was a stupid response*, his inner voice criticized.

Doc managed a more controlled, "Very well, Sir, and you?"

"Quite well boys, despite lack of sleep. I think we'll have a little rest period today so we can all catch up a little, how does that sound?"

"That sounds great to me, Captain." Ray was now more composed and he felt honored to have actually exchanged words with Thunder One. "Sir," Ray turned as the captain continued walking.

Zartman's eyes shifted to meet Ray's.

"We're really kicking ass aren't we, Sir?"

"Indeed we are son, carry on men," he said continuing aft on the main deck. The moment passed and both sailors grinned. It was like being a little kid in the presence of Superman as the legendary hero suddenly stepped out of the pages of the comic.

"Shit, Doc, that was the man! We just talked one-on-one with the big dude, Mister Thunder himself!"

"Yeah man, our buddy Zart, wait'll we tell the boys back home about this."

They slowed as they approached the officers and men loitering by turret one. Preparing to salute, they were disarmed immediately by the Executive Officer who said, "As you were men. No need to be in proper form, this is an informal gathering here."

"I have a piece of shrapnel here, Commander," Doc said holding out his hand to the XO.

The Commander took it in his fingers. "Yes, I've seen a few already. Don't you guys get in the way of any of this stuff. Do you see what it did to the turret here?" Commander Leverone was pointing aft to the scraped paint on the circular housing supporting turret two. Ray and Doc turned and looked at the site they had just walked past. It looked like someone had taken a very bent and crooked garden rake and scoured the haze gray paint down to bare metal in seven or eight places. Squiggly lines of raw metal now peeked out from behind a mask of gray.

The khakis and dungarees mingled together for some time as the men exchanged observations and comments with one another. All wore Navy blue ball caps, most with the bright yellow "NN" logo above the visor, and a few with "COMSECONDFLEET," which reminded all of the very recent, yet seemingly worlds away, past.

The sunlight grew brighter as the top of the fiery ball was emerging from the sea. As the ship headed into the rising sun, Ray bid his friend good-day and returned down the ladder aft of turret two, thinking to himself as he made his way back to Radio One, *Damn, Thunder One and Thunder Two. I've been on this ship two years and never had occasion to speak directly to either of them before.* Now there was just the watch turnover to accomplish as Bird and Don came strolling through the hatch, moments behind him.

After a brief conversation with several of the department members gathered for morning muster, Ray was ready for sleep again. Dave and Rich had been his Maincom watch counterparts through the last two nights and neither of them had talked with Ray since the action began. It was a different scene one deck above Radio One where the Teletype Center was located. Tactical communications were absent from this domain. The HF, long haul, teletype termination with one or two NAVCOMSTAs (Naval Communications Station) was the principal mode of communications here. Continual message traffic flowed over this expansive network, and part of *Newport News'* modification to a flagship had to do with this instantaneous, worldwide communications link. The carriers, other cruisers, and capital ships had these capabilities as well. The entire spectrum of message traffic was available at the twenty or so teletype machines in what was called the TTY center. Most of the personnel employed here, about eight or ten at any given time, had secret security clearances at least, with one-third of them cleared to Top Secret. Because electronically encrypted radio teletype was the most secure type of communications in the world, for any mobile unit, the majority of message traffic that was not particularly time sensitive or related directly to shipboard operations was negotiated through this link. It was a data link quite literally, not unlike today's Internet, but totally dedicated to military use. When message traffic was slow, the TTY operators often gabbed with their counterparts on the distant end, much like chatting in an Internet chat room.

For *Newport News,* in this new environment the distant end was NAVCOMSTA Subic in the Pacific Islands and alternately, NAVCOMSTA Honolulu. The TTY operators and message center clerical staff were in the process of getting to know a whole different crew of shore-based operators to shoot the breeze with during dull moments.

Inherent also in this realm were the details of pertinent messages among the heavy hitters of the military regime in the West Pacific. Situation reports (SITREPs), Intelligence Reports (INTELREPs), and Casualty Reports (CASREPs) were the most interesting, but equally important to the operations of the fleet were such things as Logistic Reports (LOGREPs) and Logistic Requests (LOGREQs), because these kept the numerous units of the Seventh Fleet supplied and coordinated.

Rich and Dave were on the senior NCO staff of the message center and, as such, were the two people who, more than anyone else, had access to all of the information passing through their space. Rich was an English Literature undergraduate who was charged with editing, proofing, and correcting documents. Dave worked with him in that realm and also on the routing process to make sure each piece of yellow teletype paper went to the proper recipient and, just as importantly, did not go elsewhere. Dave was also trained in "off-line" cryptology. Between the two of them and the duty officer of the watch, there was nothing that went in or out of the comm center that did not get their attention.

Because Ray and his Maincom buddies worked in two totally different environments, the information they received and their links to the world outside the *Newport News* were also different. When they spoke they often exchanged information. This morning was a time to catch up. Dave approached Ray while he was standing at his locker, preparing to go to the head for a shower and shave before retiring.

"Hey Ray, I've got some details on the crash yesterday. COMSEVENTHFLEET sent a CASREP out today and copied us."

"Shoot," Ray said, "I'm listening."

"Well, it was Rear Admiral Robinson, a captain named Taylor, and a Commander Leaver. They were the whole top echelon of COMCRUDESFLOT Eleven (Commander Cruiser Destroyer Flotilla)—the Admiral, his Ops Officer, Captain Taylor, and their secretary, Commander Leaver. They were the team that put the strikes together."

"Jesus, a flag officer and two major officers, that's amazing. How did that happen?"

"Well supposedly they were making a night landing on the *Providence*, I guess they were going to conduct the strikes from her. But the helo snagged something on the deck, hit the ship, and had a fire or explosion or something; anyway it went over the starboard side into the water. The ship was going like twenty knots at the time and the helo just got smashed and sank immediately. The flight crew got out and were picked up, but the admiral and his staff went down with the chopper."

"Damn, think about that, probably twenty- to thirty-year veteran major officers, just gone in a heartbeat. Isn't it strange to you how our world has completely changed in the last forty-eight hours, Dave? I mean, this all seemed like something so far away and so insignificant when we were COMSECONDFLEET. It didn't seem like there was that much happening here. We got a few stories on the news at night, and that was it. Now we're here, and it seems like everything that has happened in the last two days and nights has been a matter of life and death."

"I know what you mean, like what was all the shit going on outside the ship when we were firing? It sounded like a war out there. Austin was on the sound-powered phones in Maincom, but he couldn't figure out much of what was going on. He was freaking out I think. He muttered some profanity a couple of times and said people were reporting muzzle flashes on the beach and explosions nearby."

"Well, I can pretty much hear what's going on topside from Radio One. I have to stay tuned into all the tactical circuits to insure no outages," Ray said. "This last time I think I was catching up with a real time picture of what it was. I noticed the distinct sound of metal hitting the hull below the waterline. You can actually hear the clang it makes when a shell hits close to the hull. There's a loud, sudden thud accompanied by what sounds like someone hitting the side of a heavy, solid metal wall with a sledgehammer. Did you hear that?"

"No, sounds scary though. We just get the loud booms and a couple of things that sound like heavy spray against the hull as well as a metallic ping that was just barely perceptible. We guessed it must've been shrapnel. But it sounds ten times bigger than the biggest fireworks finale I've ever seen, just constant booms. The other ships can be heard, and it sounds like there are thousands of rounds of artillery in the air all at once."

Ray hadn't thought of it until Dave related the experience to him, but the big difference between Maincom and Radio One was that the former was above the waterline. Radio One was below the waterline. Only the armored steel hull separated Ray and his fellow crewmembers from the ocean.

Chapter 8

The War Goes On

As Ray and Dave and the rest of the night watch relaxed and fell into a long and restful sleep, the ship steamed south. Captain Zartman was sleeping peacefully in his stateroom as well. By noon, half the crew was inside the belly of the cruiser in compartments and staterooms that received no outside light except that of their now opened entry hatches. The berthing compartments and officer's staterooms were at the same level as the message center, which was two decks below the main deck, with its floor just above the waterline. There were no windows or portholes, and the steel walls of the ship's hull were about one inch thick. From the standpoint of light arms or shrapnel, these structures and the decks above them were sufficient to keep much of the crew safe unless the ship took a direct hit from armor-piercing artillery, and this was thought fairly unlikely. On the Oh-One level, above the berthing compartments, the crew's passageways ran from bow to stern with watertight hatches and stairways (ladders in shipboard talk) leading either up to the main deck or down to the berthing compartments and workspaces below. When not in proximity to the enemy, these were left open to let daylight flood in around them, giving the interior of the ship a ghostly hue approximating dusk.

Where Ray slept, in the farther recesses, removed from the hatches and toward the outer walls of the berthing compartment, it was quite dark, and most of the "old salts" used the gray wool blankets of their sleeping issue to further wall out the light. In his rack it was quiet, dark, and a comfortable sixty degrees. *Newport News* was one of the fortunate ships of the time. She had complete air conditioning for two decks below the main deck. Since the watertight hatches at the upper end of each ladder were hinged at one end and secured in their horizontal positions, only the thirty-inch circular hatch at the center of each sixty by forty-eight-inch rectangular hatch was left open for access. Thus, very little of the air-conditioned space below the main deck was affected by outside air.

The day went by quickly for those who rested here, and at 4:30 p.m. Ray woke to the sound of sporadic gunfire once again. After the first few rounds had been fired and no counter battery observed, the XO came over the 1MC with the announcement that the ship would secure General Quarters and proceed in Condition Yoke, a less severe state of readiness which allowed free movement about the ship with watertight doors and hatches only partially secured. The XO continued with an explanation that the ship had arrived at Military Region One (MR1), near Quang Tri Province, and was engaging in ground support NGFS (naval gunfire support) operations for forces inland. He followed this with the information that: "We are slated to remain here for several days while the South Vietnamese forces make an amphibious assault on Viet Cong forces north of and engaged with defenders at the seventeenth parallel, otherwise known as the Demilitarized Zone, or DMZ; the supposed border between the forces of North and South Vietnam."

Operation Freedom Train was the name of this campaign. It was slower paced at the outset than what the Task Group had experienced in the four strike raids of the past two nights. Now attached to Task Unit 70.8.9, the *Newport News* was in the company of several dozen other cruisers and destroyers cruising within two or three miles of the Vietnam Coast. Not steaming, but with her boilers at the ready, she was moving slowly and drifting listlessly at times, while intermittently firing missions requested by spotters and troops on the shore.

After dressing and visiting the head for his wakeup constitutional, Ray went topside and strolled the deck. He had another hour and a half before relieving Bird in Radio One, and now a completely new aspect of their experience was unfolding.

The weather was perfect, with a bright afternoon sun one and a half hours above the horizon. There were ships all around as far, and in every direction, as he could see. Most were destroyers, but a few cruisers and frigates were in company as well, some in the act of firing short bursts of gunfire at inland targets that were indiscernible from this range. The interesting thing to Ray was that most of them were situated in what looked like a totally askew formation—a bow pointing here or there randomly as they used whatever gun system was called for at the moment. Most of the destroyers were pointing toward the beach at various angles employing their forward five-inch thirty-eight twin or single mounts. (The newer ships had single barrel five-inch rapid fire mounts while the older, World War II vintage destroyers used twin five-inch mounts exactly like the secondary batteries on the *Newport News*.)

Ray noted the huge inequality between these two different classes of ships. The destroyers and slightly larger frigates of the post World War II era had one, sometimes two, forward five-inch mounts and one at the rear. This was their main battery. The newer ships, like the nuclear powered frigate *Bainbridge*, had a single five-inch mount forward and Talos missile launchers at the rear. His observations, however, had not detected any missile launches so far, and only the sporadic gun bursts were evident. None of the ships were any closer than perhaps one-half mile from any of the others, and each seemed to be doing its own thing. It was curious at first, but also closer to what Ray had expected of Vietnam.

The Radio One watch that evening was much less eventful than the previous two nights. The ship remained at Condition Yoke, and watch team members moved about taking breaks to go topside and view the ongoing slow-moving shelling.

Radio traffic on the tactical command circuits had morphed into sporadic but continuing calls and responses between the many ships of Task Group 70.8.9 and their spotters on shore occasionally interspersed with urgent calls from ground troops conducting reconnaissance missions in preparation for the big push scheduled for the next morning. The rumor mill within CR Division came to life again; through the night Ray kept getting updates from Dave, Rich, and Chief Yerks.

Apparently, Operation Freedom Train was going to include a massive amphibious assault where the Navy would insert 5,000 South Vietnamese Army and Marine troops, by helicopter, into positions around enemy strongholds north of the DMZ. The shelling that was occurring at present was to take out enemy artillery emplacements and bunkers where the VC had become entrenched and fortified. A select group of reconnaissance specialists composed of Navy and Marine Corps SEALs and their South Vietnamese counterparts were working the area in specialized teams ahead of the main event.

The voice radio traffic was interesting to Ray and Mike as they worked through the night. Occasionally, each would take a topside break to go up and see what could be seen. The crew had been instructed to stay aft of amidships for the night since *Newport News* was employing both of her forward turrets in her firing missions. As Ray stepped out onto the main deck at 3:15 a.m., the Cruiser *Providence* was firing several salvos from its forward six-inch gun turret. She was about one-third of a mile south of *Newport News'* position and perhaps half a mile off the beach. *Ka-Wham* went the report of her cannons coming seconds behind the brilliant, reddish-white flash. A few seconds later another flash and the delayed boom rattled the superstructure of Ray's surroundings once again. *Jesus!* Ray thought to himself, *that's a three shot salvo from one six-inch turret. I wonder what our eight-inchers must be like when turrets one and two are firing simultaneous salvos.*

He didn't have long to wait—without warning, *Ba-Boom, Ba-Boom!* The sound made Ray jump as the forward half of the ship was illuminated in bright light. Flames shot out to the starboard side of the ship a distance of about forty feet as the ear-splitting report fell silent. In the two thunderous volleys, twelve eight-inch projectiles hurled inland as turrets one and two fired in synchronization. The fifty or so off-duty sailors milling about on the after main deck responded with expressions of awe and excitement; war-whoops and expletives erupted almost involuntarily as the men experienced the fury of this scene.

Ray stepped back inside the Radio One hatch at about 3:30. Mike knew something had happened from the look on his face. "What did you see Ray?"

"Jesus Mike, you wouldn't believe it, those things are incredible!"

"I just heard the spotters talking to the bridge. We just wiped out a few NVA tanks that were dug in fairly close to one another. The spotters said they were blown to bits along with some enemy troops. Think about it, twelve 500-pound bombs coming out of nowhere. Those guys are about fifteen miles away. Man, there's no way I would ever want to be on the receiving end of that shit," Mike replied.

"You said it buddy, not a good time to be a North Vietnamese soldier."

The night continued with occasional firings. Those asleep in their bunks awakened numerous times, but already began to realize that this would become more routine. Many had begun an acclimation process that would allow them to sleep right through the noise and vibration almost without stirring.

Chapter 9

Message of the B-52s

Ray was sleeping soundly after a good meal and a few minutes of relaxation. He had walked the main deck forward to the mid-ship hatch after breakfast, and observed that the fleet of ships remained much as it was the prior afternoon, though it was now shrouded in the morning fog. The only difference was that no ships appeared to be firing. Was it the calm before the storm?

One and a half hours into his sleep in his dark, cool, comfortable rack just inches off the floor, he was in dreamland enjoying a far away interlude with Cynthia in a field of wildflowers on a bright, sunny summer day. It was bliss. They were in love.

Slowly his mind came into the consciousness of the present. Gradually, and then more quickly, the dream faded and his senses became tuned to something foreign. The ship was vibrating—a continual, unfamiliar rumbling. It grew more intense as his eyes opened sleepily. Concerned voices emanated from some of the other bunks. He heard the slapping of bare feet on tiled floors as men got out of their bunks in haste. It felt like the entire ship was resonating now with a vibration much like standing near a railroad track as a freight train raced past. It was similar to the way it felt to be standing on the fantail when the ship was steaming at flank speed, only this was throughout the whole ship. What was happening?

What the hell is going on, he thought. *No guns were firing, no bursts like explosions from counter battery. There was no sudden movement like the ship was maneuvering quickly, in fact the ship seemed still except for the continual and increasing vibration. What was it? Was the ship on fire? Was it being rattled by small arms fire?*

Ray rose form his bunk and grabbed his shower togs, wrapping them around his waist and buttoning them on. He began to walk toward the companionway hatch where others were congregating and beginning to move up the stairs. The men looked around in startled concern, and begin to ask one another, “What’s going on?” Ray had reached the foot of the compartment stairway when the speakers crackled to life.

The XOs voice came over the 1MC: “What you’re feeling now are the effects of a three plane B-52 raid on Quang Tri City, fifteen miles inland.” The XOs words hung in silence at first, then involuntary exclamations erupted throughout the compartment. *Holy shit*, was all Ray could think at the moment. *Three B-52s fifteen miles inland and then across two miles of ocean causing a 21,000-ton cruiser to vibrate like a child’s toy in a bathtub? Am I dreaming? This can’t be real!* The exclamations rose, accompanied by whistles of amazement and other startled responses.

Ray was not dreaming. As they came to know later, each of the heavy bombers carried 105 500-pound bombs. When they unleashed their fury on a single target, in unison, the effect of 315 bombs hitting the ground in less than one minute was inconceivable for anyone but those who fell in or near the target area—and for miles in all directions. Even the dense jungle and the mountainous coastal terrain did not muffle the energy release. Seventeen miles away and this extreme power still had the ability to shake the fleet of ships sitting off the coast of Vietnam. The repercussions were stronger and louder than the most violent thunderstorm could have produced directly overhead.

For some, the immediate response was to think about the difference between the distance they were feeling it at and being at the direct place where all this energy was unleashed; it was mind-boggling, simply incomprehensible, absolutely overwhelming. Faint tears appeared at the corner of some of their eyes as they realized there was carnage and horror happening in this world, right now, in this very moment within mere miles of their position. Whatever the number or appearance of any humans under that consuming force might be, whatever god or higher power they might believe in, one thing was very certain—they had to be meeting their maker at this very instant.

So far, Newport News had been in the war zone for about sixty hours. She had fired 323 rounds of eight-inch and five-inch artillery at the enemy during four strike raids before arriving at MR1. That was about equivalent to what the B-52s had done in just one minute. My God! Ray thought.

Newport News made up one of five Task Unit elements in each of those raids, and her singular firepower was equivalent to about one-third of the entire Task Group. The numbers and magnitudes of the forces working in this extremely complex physics problem were beyond Ray’s comprehension, but essentially it looked like the force of one of the strike raids up North was similar to what had just been done by the B-52s. And that was unimaginable to him. *We're devastating them with incredible power,* he thought, and he kept turning that over and over in his mind.

Eventually, he fell back into a deep sleep until 5:00 p.m. when the firing of a few short missions stirred him once again.

It was late afternoon, May 13. He checked the calendar as he walked by the large card table and chairs that were always present at the entranceway to the CR Division berthing compartment. On his way up to the Oh-One level passageway he again contemplated the morning's event.

The ship was now at Condition Yoke continuously. Ray headed to the mess decks for coffee and a meal. Afterward, there would be one and a half hours to go topside and observe the war before watch.

Readiness Condition Yoke was less cumbersome, in terms of moving about the ship, than General Quarters Condition Zebra. Instead of having all watertight doors and hatches closed and fully secured, during Yoke every other hatch or door, thus fifty percent of them, were secured. This allowed movement about the ship without having to open any of the secured hatches and doors, but, in order to accomplish this, a person had to choose his route using only the unsecured barriers. This made Ray's route indirect. The purpose in doing this was to reduce by half the amount of time and energy required to bring the ship to Condition Zebra should an enemy threat become more severe.

The next several days were spent in Military Region One. The fire missions became more numerous and a number of interesting events were interspersed among periods of slow, sometimes boring time. Ray, Bird, and Doc had a few relaxation periods listening to music in the ECCM room.

The ships came and went, each on a predetermined schedule worked out by teams of planners who used the communications links CR Division made available to them. In this realm, now that interdepartmental relations had become more open, there was a sense among more and more of the crew that they were living in a real life or death environment. The night action up north was still fresh in their minds and the specter of future raids loomed in their thoughts. They began, just slightly, to become closer (the pulling together that is often referred to when combat veterans speak of their brethren) and more open with one another. It progressed slowly; soon there were more conversations between members of different departments. The operations people talked more freely with technicians in the ship's engineering, supply, weapons, and communications departments.

There were many news resources in CR Division. Along with the constant teletype traffic and voice radio networks, the ship could monitor a vast number of media links concerning real time events. The wire services, UPI, and AP ran constant networks of world news which *Thunder* was plugged into. There were several military news resources as well. Armed Forces Radio and Television Network, AFRTS (pronounced "A-farts" by the sailors) was a news media supplied by the government to the general population of service personnel. At the time, news-reel footage was common and this was distributed around the fleet. Supplementing this were regional radio broadcasts from places in the north and south of Vietnam. Saigon and DaNang AFRTS stations could be heard as well as broadcasts from Hanoi, which came and went with the atmospheric conditions.

For the Radio One personnel there was plenty of work to keep them busy. Tactical voice networks were continually rotating through a long list of frequencies to insure none was used for a particular application long enough for enemy technicians to glean information from it. The crypto equipment as well was continually cycled through a myriad of key codes. Each time these were changed, the content that went out on the airwaves was re-scrambled in a different way.

Inherent to these activities was the continual re-tuning, adjusting, and rotating for maintenance of perhaps one hundred or so transmitters and transceivers located in five or six separate radio equipment rooms around the ship. Different crews within CR Division accomplished these things. Other men like Swanny, Woody, and Jeff worked with transmitter and antenna equipment.

Another source of continual effort was the cross training of various skills, which helped to solidify efficiency and cooperation among the division's human resources. The overall communications and radio world was a continual work in progress arranged very well by its officers.

For the rest of May and into the first part of June the cruiser stayed in MR1. There were interludes about every third day when she headed out to the support fleet for ammo, fuel, and supplies. These diversions would take from two to four hours each way, ranging in distance from approximately fifty to one hundred miles east of the Gun-line.

The rest of the time, firing missions went on for twenty-four hours every day. At times, the fire would be furious in short spurts, but most often there were long periods of silence. There were several instances of counter battery from the beach, usually consisting of one or two airbursts in the general proximity of the ship, but no casualties were taken.

The information passing throughout the crew by the beginning of June became more specific. There were stories of tanks and troops being stopped or destroyed. The first operation of Freedom Train that had started on May 16, known as "Song Than 5-72," had fizzled. Reports from the beach indicated that after several days the 5,000 South Vietnamese soldiers airlifted in to stem the tide of North Vietnamese had been largely decimated, many of them leaving their weapons and running home. This was one of the first big offensive actions to be undertaken by the South since the Vietnamization of the war. It was beginning to look as though our Asian brothers were not competent, or perhaps not confident, without their American compatriots.

News footage of the battle for Quang Tri Province was now being received on the television sets that made up the central focus of the eight-by-sixteen-foot common area at the entrance to each berthing compartment. The photos of Quang Tri City were unimaginable. There were no buildings left in the city that had been home to several hundred thousand South Vietnamese before the siege. Nothing but rubble could be seen. On clear days, the men, though fifteen miles away, could see a pall of smoke rising tens of thousands of feet into the atmosphere and appearing to continue into outer space. When the wind was off-shore, the faint smell of earth and burned flesh wafted to the warships.

When the occasional "pot-shot" from VC gunners appeared in an airburst near the flotilla, the scene felt threatening to the sailors occupying the topside spaces. Occasionally, when the harassment persisted, an air strike by Huey Cobras or Fighter Jets would curtail it. The men heard that the gook gunners had tunnels dug into the hills east of the target zone and would roll their 130mm field cannons out to rattle off a few rounds, then haul them back into the cave before they could be spotted and engaged. On one occasion, a couple of Cobra crews were stationed behind the crest of the high ground where the gunners had been detected. They waited and when the artillery pieces began to fire again, they rose up over the hill and pounced on them. Sailors with binoculars or particularly acute vision viewed this scene from the ships.

Ray could only conceive of a swarm of angry hornets as he watched the two tiny dots pour out what looked like solid streams of fire into a blossoming dust cloud on the shore. Swaying back and forth in a near hover, but moving side to side in an arch, the two Hueys devastated their adversary. The word came back to the ships that this VC gun emplacement had been silenced.

Ray had difficulty thinking about all of this. As the spotter plane responsible for the strike flew out to buzz the ships, the sailors cheered. The small twin-boom military version of a Cessna Skymaster hopped about the fleet wagging its wings and circling in what was unmistakable jubilation on the part of its pilot.

Ray shared in this feeling, but at the same time tried hard to imagine the scene on the beach—a small team, perhaps four or five men, rolling their piece out in what had become routine for them, firing several rounds, and then suddenly finding themselves accosted by two angry and nimble gun ships appearing out of nowhere. Two 6,000-round-per-minute .30 caliber mini-guns shattered their very being into bits of flesh and steel.

He thought about Brian, the motionless, lifeless body lying in full dress uniform in his coffin. He knew Brian had been killed in a firefight too. His prime, well-conditioned body had been penetrated by the same fusillade of bullets and shrapnel these North Vietnamese soldiers had been "silenced" by. All of them had been taken unawares and suddenly terminated in the peak of their youth. Whatever their philosophy or allegiance, all who died in combat reached the same end. It was sad to think about the friends and relatives of those four or five men who would now experience the same loss and the same emptiness that Brian's death had caused Ray's family.

As he contemplated this, he was not yet aware of the dichotomy developing in his mind. *Well, you mess with the United States of America, and you will get what's coming to you*, he rationalized. *This is War.*

It was war to him and to the others who shared this domain. Some of the cruisers and destroyers in this present Task Group had never seen anything but the present situation, and did not, in fact, even know about the strikes up north. For them, the situation here in MR1 was "war." Others out farther, in places like Yankee station, knew war as the constant recycling of aircraft from their flight decks to targets in the north or south. In these scenarios, only the crews of their aircraft were actually experiencing "combat." Additionally, and not to be downplayed, were the experiences of the members of the "service fleet" who saw only the re-supply and rearming of combatant units arriving and departing their vicinity. Most of them lived continually under dangerous conditions, with their constant handling of thousands of tons of munitions, fuel, and supplies progressing at a breakneck pace. All who contributed to these operations knew, at some level, there were people dying due to their efforts to "hold the line."

The special operations units, sailors, and Marines who manned the Riverine boat patrols along with Vietnamese ground troops saw war at another level of combat. To them, it was up close and personal. They were "inserted" and "extracted" often and, at times, took casualties. More often though, they dispatched the enemy with incredible efficiency. Here again, the technological superiority of our side was undeniable. Kill ratios for the entire effort were considered to be hundreds, or even thousands, to one.

To the men of *Newport News* and the other members of TG 70.1.1, the slower pace of shelling the enemy in support missions here in the vicinity of the DMZ was much less "combat-like" than what they had experienced several nights ago. When they left MR1 on June 26, they had fired another 3,723 rounds of eight-inch and 2,129 rounds of five-inch ammunition, rearmed numerous times, and gone through several replenishment operations. They had also logged sixty-two more rounds of hostile fire from enemy artillery and gotten away without a scratch.

Chapter 10

When Giants are Close

On the 26th of May, *Newport News* was scheduled to rearm and refuel from the service fleet once more and head north to meet with TU 77.1.1. The surface gunfire and aircraft strike missions had now collectively become known as "Operation Linebacker." The purpose defined in the strike plans and intelligence reports indicated that the U.S. was now projecting maximum effort against the North by the Navy and Air Force. The military hoped this would erode the command and control capabilities of the VC in South Vietnam, interrupt their supply logistics, and demoralize the enemy.

There were now three to five heavy aircraft carriers on Yankee Station at any given time. Each with ninety or so aircraft, they generated an armada-size operation of air sorties continuing around the clock. The cruiser/destroyer flotillas were the next wave inward, working the immediate shoreline and targets as far as their guns and missiles could reach inland. Closer in still were the special operations units, SEALs and riverine strike units, taking on the more personal task of intelligence gathering and interdiction of enemy units that required direct search and destroy or capture and interrogate efforts. Maincom personnel, like Dave and Kent, now leaked freely details on these matters to others in the comm crew. The circle of secrecy was widening as time passed.

Along with all these Naval resources, the Air Force was carrying the war to the north from surrounding bases in Southeast Asia. Many previous "potential" targets that had been considered "out of bounds" or "immune" were being reassessed and put on strike plans. Most were re-categorized as vital targets.

The day before heading back up north, *Newport News* received a team of six who had been evacuated from their electronic snoop base near the DMZ. These CTs joined the three from SuppRad and became the "guests" of the Navy for the present. These men bunked in CR

Division with the radiomen. Their presence was immediately felt. They were quite agitated and traumatized by the situation that had precipitated their sudden extraction. One of them, Denny, appeared to be one or two years older than Ray, very intelligent and in peak physical condition. In conversing with Denny, Ray had found him willing, even wanting, to tell about his experiences.

It had been harrowing. They had been warding off an increasing level of sniper activity for several weeks and, on the 24th of May, North Vietnamese soldiers had overrun their position. They lost two team members immediately and held their ground until Huey gunships and transport helos had airlifted them out to the fleet.

Ray talked with Denny for some time, finding out that he was an ex-Marine who had served two former tours in Vietnam and worked as a communications technician. Denny had been directly involved in listening, analyzing, and interfering with enemy radio traffic. He spoke every regional dialect and was familiar with the lexicons of the military people in the Vietnam, Cambodia, and Thailand region. He had served in numerous places in-country and had seen a great deal of the "black" realm of covert government operations

Denny had been involved at some level with the Vietnam War since 1968. After finishing his undergraduate education at UCLA at the age of twenty, he had spent four years in the Marine Corps before accepting a position with an intelligence agency, but was not at liberty to say exactly who signed his paychecks. During rotations back to the states he attended further courses and achieved a Masters in Political Science with an emphasis on Asian Politics and a second degree in Linguistics.

Denny's path at the age of twenty-five had been much different than Ray's. He had lived in the San Diego area all his life and was the son of an Admiral whose forbearers had made up the military elite for several generations. The Marine had been an extremely intelligent and fiercely patriotic youth who had graduated high school at the age of fourteen in the "accelerated learning environment" of the progressive society of the west coast. He began college immediately and was accepted into the Navy's O.C.S. program when he reached the age of seventeen, with his parents' blessing. His military education, adjunct to the university's programs, included training in a broad spectrum of communications technology and further conditioning in the secret world of covert military operations. He had trained with the special warfare group at Coronado Island and was a capable soldier as well as a major intellect.

Denny would become one of Ray's greatest sources of information about the real events and the state of things as they developed in Southeast Asia. It occurred to Ray once again that he was working in a very privileged society. The information resources available and, to a degree, necessary in his occupation gave him a perspective that was denied the majority of enlisted personnel.

Here, once again, Ray felt a sense of surrealism. It was as though he had a private window; he looked out on events like an observer having prior knowledge of the details. At times he imagined himself in the control room of a TV network during the coverage of a major sporting event. Like the engineer of a broadcast crew on Super bowl Sunday, he took the information flooding into the comm center and dealt with each piece as required. Some would require immediate action on his part, some would be passed on in any of a myriad of ways to those whose attention they required, and some just filled the blanks of his awareness in a given moment. He was in the loop at many junctures, and that was a good place to be.

In two week's time the entire crew of *Thunder* had become well adjusted to the new role they were playing in the West Pacific. Their training and the events in this short period had taken on a new level of importance to them all. Now, a majority of the men were psyched for the challenges that lay ahead. The term "Gung Ho" was becoming more personal to them; they started talking in terms of "killing gooks" as though the use of the phrase made them each that much tougher.

Ray walked the main deck in the early afternoon of the 26th enjoying the sunshine, the crystal blue water of the South China Sea, and a mild breeze. It was eighty-five degrees or so, and humid. The sea and sky blended together at the horizon, and a few puffy white clouds drifted by as the ship made its way to the north. Walking forward on the port side, Ray ran across Bird standing at the outboard edge near the portside forward five-inch gun mount. He was smoking a cigarette and scratching his chin thoughtfully. Ray stepped toward his friend and greeted him.

"Hey Bird, what's up?" Bird shot him a glance as he flicked the cigarette butt over the side into the churning sea.

"Not much, dude, how 'bout you?"

"Oh, same shit, different day," Ray answered. "Anything new from the rumor mill?"

"Well, I had a pretty interesting detail to work on this morning; the Chief had me go up to SuppRad. The new guys up there brought a bunch of equipment with them that hadn't had any maintenance performed on it for some time, so he had me inventory it and schedule it for PMS (Preventive Maintenance Service). I got to see the inside of that place and meet some of the guys that work there. Pretty intriguing stuff."

"I've been talking to Denny. Did you know that guy is a political scientist and linguist? He's got a Masters in Political Science in Asian affairs and also speaks every Asian dialect known to man. He says there are a lot of different local variations here in Southeast Asia."

"Well I know when I was up there the people working were talking in gook both on the air and to one another. Seemed pretty strange, a group of Americans speaking gook. Hey, you know we could probably go up there if you want to check it out, there's not much happening in One right now. We're in transit for the day."

"Sure, I'd love to check it out, let's go."

Ray and Bird walked aft through a watertight door on the portside superstructure and began climbing the stairway in the same general vicinity they were familiar with when going to Doc's ECCM space. Another deck above and several yards aft of the ECCM room another door broke out onto the catwalk running aft along the superstructure of the ship. They stopped at a door with no markings; Ray noticed it had a large, secure-looking lock hasp on it and an equally rugged combination lock hanging from it. The hasp was open and there were muted sounds coming from within. Bird knocked on the door and after a span of several seconds it opened. The figure standing on the other side poked his head out, squinting in the bright daylight.

"Hi, I'm RM3 Burdulis. I was here earlier working on some of your equipment. This is RM3 Kopp. He's giving me a hand on this project."

"Oh yes," the bespectacled face responded, "c'mon in."

Bird and Ray stepped into the dimly lit, windowless room as the door clanged shut behind them, its deadbolt slamming home with a whack.

"I just wanted to show Ray around," Bird said, "he's never been up here before and we had a little time, so thought I'd orient him with the space and the gear up here."

As their eyes became adjusted to the light, Ray could make out four or five figures dressed in olive drab utilities peering at electronic equipment and reading from publications, some of which were stamped with the familiar "SECRET" security code. As his eyes swept back and forth he noticed Denny's familiar face. Denny shot him a look of recognition as he continued making adjustments to a piece of electronic equipment.

Ray could see oscilloscopes, frequency spectrum analyzers, and numerous receiver and antenna tuning panels. The place looked a lot like Radio One, only it was about one-third the size and manned by five people. There were audio sounds similar to his workspace and, from time to time, voices speaking in Vietnamese would burst over one of several speakers mounted on the bulkhead. The comm-techs were listening intently to the radio conversations. Now and then they would repeat and restructure the remarks they heard, as if for clarification among themselves.

Bird and Ray just observed without speaking. It was clear that these men did not want to be distracted. Bird pointed Ray in the direction of some portable radio equipment that was bundled together in one end of the room, and they strode toward it.

"Oh yeah," Ray muttered in a low tone so as not to disturb the ongoing activities, "PRC-25s with KY-14s attached." The equipment was familiar, but unlike the portable secure voice radio sets he had just become familiar with, these showed signs of usage and wear. One of the radios even had a groove in it, which Ray immediately recognized as the mark a bullet makes when encountering the surface of a piece of sheet steel. He ran his finger across the groove. "This looks like a .30 caliber rifle ricochet to me. Bird, what do you think?"

"I can't say I'd know what one looks like, but it sure as hell got hit by something." The two sailors observed the scene in SuppRad for some time before Bird glanced at his watch and said, "Hey, I have to get back down to One. I'm sure Don is ready for a break by now."

"OK, buddy. Well, this has been very interesting for sure."

The two friends exited the room with a wave to the occupants and stepped back into the bright sunlight. As they scanned the horizon, Bird noticed a ship several miles away to their forward port quarter. "Looks like we're going to get some ammo before we go any farther," he said, looking at the lumbering ship in the distance.

"Yeah, that's an AE (ammunition ship) all right," Ray responded.

Once down on the main deck the two parted ways and Ray continued his relaxing stroll around the teakwood expanse. The waves lapped at the waterline as he bent to look over the side. The ship was slowing now to maneuver into position alongside the AE, still several miles off. It occurred to Ray that the physics involved in such stuff was immense—21,000-tons of ship maneuvering into position alongside another whose mass was probably twice that carrying a huge cargo of explosive ordinance. The forces imparted by each of these giants had to be controlled so skillfully and with such precision that it boggled his mind. Before the two ships could pass the high lines between each other, they had to be in sync with respect to speed and direction, and also had to be within about twenty yards; only then could the transfer of ammo begin. Ray decided to hang out and watch since he had some time to kill. He had already observed a number of underway replenishments, but now he could actually take the time to study the process.

As this event unfolded before his eyes, Ray watched and, at the same time, made a comparison between what he was seeing here in broad daylight and what his conceptual picture of the night raids up north had been like. It occurred to him that his role as a communications person was linked to both of these situations. Here in the bright sunshine, the surrounding deep blue sea, and the frothy white wakes of the two ships merging as they rendezvoused, it seemed quite mundane and harmless. The logistical communications needed in this process were routine and, to a large extent, seldom consciously thought about by their users. On the bridge the Officer of the deck and his crew communicated with the ammunition ship as if talking on the telephone to one's neighbor, with the exception of proper military jargon and circuit discipline. Signalmen stood on the promenade outboard of the bridge where the captain and XO observed the operation. The signalmen's flags were waving semaphore instructions as a backup to the radio link.

Sailors on both ships waved and shouted salutations as the distance between these two steel monsters closed. Lead lines were shot across the expanse of roiling water between the ships after their positions had been stabilized. The bosons that raised the shoulder-held guns to perform this act stood tall as though it was their finest hour, belying the humdrum of this thankless job they had done for days and months on end.

The *USS Vesuvious* was dirty and grungy looking, in contrast to what Ray had been used to in his Second Fleet duty. It occurred to him for the first time that most of the Seventh Fleet ships looked the same. *The difference between the wartime and peacetime Navy*, he thought. A ship and her crew in a war zone constantly at sea and working long, strenuous days and nights did not have much time for aesthetic concerns. The sailors lined the weather decks watching intently as those involved in the high line transfer continued their work. It was apparent that many of them were impressed. They motioned and called to one another and pointed in the direction of the heavy cruiser. *It wasn't often they experienced the view of a major league gunship*, he thought. Their imaginations were probably running wild with wonder at what exactly this fearsome leviathan would do once she was again over the western horizon off the coast of Vietnam.

At the same time, he tried to gauge the awesome destructive potential that would be unleashed if either of these two great ships were to turn, however slightly, in the direction of the other, even at this relatively benign speed of ten knots. A collision between two large ships would be catastrophic. Applying that realization to the Task Unit Strike operations, Ray found himself overwhelmed. *Wow!* his mind snapped into focus, *what if we collided with the* OK City *or the* Providence *while zigzagging into a strike raid in total darkness at thirty knots!* It put the real importance of communications into a whole new light for him. "Son-of-a-bitch," the words fell aloud from his mouth as a cold chill ran down the back of his neck.

Rearming at sea

Two large steel cables, one fore and one aft, were strung between the two ships now. Propped up with heavy steel tripods, these were held about twenty feet above the main deck of each ship. The tension was held and adjusted by teams of sailors on each ship who maintained the cables at a constant height as the ships rocked slowly back and forth, each to its own rhythm with the sea. Ray watched for a while as the *Vesuvious* and her crew passed pallets of bullets, in the form of eight-inch and five-inch artillery shells, to the cruiser. He observed for an hour or so before returning to the berthing compartment. Once there, he wrote Cynthia a letter and spent some quiet time before dinner and his evening duty. A couple of hours later he heard the announcement over the 1MC: “Secure the rearming detail, now set the normal underway watch.” *Off again to the war*, he thought to himself, realizing that it had become commonplace to him. But he had forgotten for a moment the great difference between the past couple of weeks down south and what was coming with the approaching evening.

His mind drifted back again to the scene in SuppRad earlier. I wonder what those guys are doing there, he thought to himself; do they talk to the gooks? Are they feeding them misinformation? Are they faking them out, screwing with their minds? That must be fascinating work! I’m gonna see what I can dig out of Denny the next time I see him.

Chapter 11

Killing Hits Home

Ray and Mike, along with Chief Yerks, were on watch for one hour when, at 8:00 p.m., the captain brought the ship to General Quarters again for only the second time in the last two weeks.

"This is the captain speaking," the 1MC speakers came to life throughout the ship. "We've been sitting pretty down south for a while now and, with only a few exceptions, we've been relatively unchallenged by the enemy. I think we've logged only four or five instances of counter battery aimed at us in the last ten days, with none of those coming close enough to cause concern. I want to commend everyone for the work we've done thus far. As you all no doubt realize, the Navy is having no trouble finding work for us here, and there is no shortage of firing missions in Military Region One. The northern border of Quang Tri Province is the front line in this phase of the war, and there's a lot happening there. With that said, it's time to take this ship back up to Charlie's home turf and raise a little hell before we go back to Subic for a few days rest. It's going to be pretty much like the first few nights we were here, and I know some of you guys are itching to get your adrenaline levels back up, so this will be your opportunity. I want to remind everyone to stay alert and ready at all times. Keep your peckers up!"

It was as if the mere mention of the word adrenaline made it happen on command. Ray and the others in Radio One began to feel alert, confident, and eager to get on with the raid.

For this night, there were four ships in close formation, Task Group 77.1.1 was only slightly different in its structure than 77.1.2. Instead of three cruisers and two destroyers, there were now only two cruisers and two smaller ships. The night was dark again. The speed and agility of the flotilla's movements became foremost in each of the sailors' consciousness and seemed familiar in a welcome sort of way. The noises of rapidly moving mechanical servos and very terse messages over the tactical command radio circuits added to the charged feeling in Radio One.

It was like the feeling of going up the first hill on a really scary roller coaster ride, Ray thought to himself. The excitement built as the realization flooded into his mind, and, once begun, there was no stopping it. *Danger!* his inner consciousness signaled as his mouth became dry and his heart rate increased. He heard the TG Commander's voice calling the last turn before the firing leg, and then everything broke loose with a fury he had not experienced since two weeks earlier.

"Holy Shit!" he exclaimed involuntarily at the sounds of the fusillade of outgoing artillery. Mike and the Chief looked at Ray's wide opened eyes and grinned back at him with a devilish gleam in their own. The Chief punched his fist skyward in a visual exclamation of satisfaction. A perceptible rally of voices came filtering through the air from classified control and over the sound powered phone circuit. Short bursts of static momentarily interrupted the tactical secure voice circuit when the salvos fired. Ray remembered this glitch from the first raids and again noted its potential significance, scanning the status boards and visually noting the backup equipment waiting to be patched into any circuit that experienced a malfunction. *This would be a hell of a time to lose communications with the rest of the Task Group*, he thought to himself.

Then came the sound of the five-inchers banging away at defensive artillery on the beach. More shouts of "give 'em hell" and "take that you gook motherfuckers" came right on the heels of their distinct reports. Again, the scene turned surreal to Ray. *Jesus*, he thought, *this is what it's really all about. This is why I'm here, God damn it. Die you motherfucking gooks!*

As in the earlier raids, the action faded away with the distant thuds of counter battery. The incoming shells had not come very close this time; there were no distinct metallic pings or sledgehammer bangs like they had heard before. The men had some time to calm down and regroup before going back a couple of hours later.

During the slack time, Ray began to realize how much things had changed since that first night in Haiphong. The difference between this and the gunfire support role the ship played down south was immense. In the south there were lots of firing missions, but these were undertaken only when needed by the troops operating inland and out of view. It was difficult to imagine what they were actually experiencing. The sailors could rarely catch a glimpse of the action; often it was ten to twenty miles off. Occasionally there would be the excited voice of a spotter on the ground or in one of the many spotter aircraft that conveyed the seriousness of the operations, but for the most part it was like being far off and away from the center of action.

The *Newport News* had fired 3,698 rounds of eight-inch shells, 2,129 rounds of five-inch shells, and had taken 216 rounds of incoming artillery from the enemy since arriving in Military Region One. There had been reports of pulverized tanks and trucks, numerous dead bodies, explosions of ammo bunkers and fuel caches, and much praise sent back to *Thunder* by appreciative grunts on the beach and commanders of various operations. Nothing that felt particularly threatening had occurred in Military Region One.

One day when the ship was returning from a refueling and rearming rendezvous, an unexpected GQ was called and the men all scrambled for their battle stations. The word soon got around that there had been unidentified aircraft, detected by radar, which looked ominous as though they were heading for the cruiser. But these turned away before getting close enough to attack. It was theorized they might have been North Vietnamese MIGs, but the other possibility was they were friendly "non-squawkers." A non-squawker referred to any aircraft not transmitting its transponder code. The military used a system called IFF, "Identification Friend/Foe," to separate its aircraft from the enemy's. Sometimes because of equipment malfunctions or bureaucratic mix-ups, our own aircraft would be either unable to or instructed not to use its identification systems.

Moreover, the slower pace and intermittent nature of the missions down south had allowed the relatively "green" crew of *Newport News* to acclimate to the war zone's busy working schedules and the warrior mentality that prevailed throughout this region. This reality, however, somehow tended to seem anti-climactic after starting out with the Haiphong and Do Son Peninsula Raids. Many of the men began to think these had been an aberration that would seldom be repeated.

Down south, it got boring at times. Things seemed to progress very slowly. It was tedious, there was very little excitement, and often it was hard to find things to do to stay occupied. You could only write so many letters, watch so many film-clips, play so many games of spades, drink so many cokes, and take so many pictures of rearming and refueling details and the other ships in the fleet. The only positive side of the situation was the fact that, because everyone worked a twelve-hour shift, the men were all weary at the end of their watches and did not find it hard to sleep when bedtime rolled around. And they had, after a fashion, become quite accomplished at sleeping through fire missions since these continued around the clock.

On the other hand, here in the north it was exciting. You felt alive, you felt challenged, you knew there were people out there who were aiming big artillery at you and trying to take you out while you were making that impossible for them and, instead, taking them out. It felt like power, it felt like invincibility, it felt like victory, it felt like getting even. And then, just for one moment, an ever-so-fleeting moment, it occurred to Ray that it felt like killing.

Ray had known killing before. He'd been a hunter since the age of twelve. He'd killed woodchucks, squirrels, grouse, a Canada goose once, raccoons, rabbits, even deer. This was a part of growing up in the country—everyone did it, and it was accepted. Being resourceful enough to know how to live off the land and its wildlife, if necessary, was honorable. His people never made waste of their wildlife harvests and their pursuits were a source of pride. *After all*, he thought*, the Native Americans had survived this way for centuries*. He had also caught and killed many trout. Beautiful and pristine as all of these creatures were, he had gutted them, cleaned them, taken them home, and eaten them for supper. In his way of thinking, that was a valid way in which to truly appreciate them, God's bounty; there was nothing unusual about it.

He had seen dead people before too, some in caskets in funeral homes. On one occasion his father and brother had been summoned to an accident scene. Before the days of emergency squads and first responders, it was not unusual for some of the townspeople to be called out to assist in an emergency. On this occasion, three freight haulers had lost the brakes on their fully loaded tractor-trailer rig coming down a steep dirt road and crashed into a ravine near town. When the two older men and fourteen-year-old Ray arrived on the scene to help their neighbors, there was one dead body lying in the creek bed and a seriously injured person trapped in the cab of the truck.

He had also lost two high school friends who died violently in a car accident while drinking one night after a friendly football game. Plus there was Brian's death, and two sailors who had fallen overboard during his earlier time aboard the *Newport News,* and yet another on this cruise.

He had seen death all through his formative years right up to the past two and a half years in the Navy, so it wasn't as though he had never experienced killing or death before; he knew it and realized its finality. But, for one reason or another, this felt different.

No sooner had the thought occurred to him than it was gone. The Task Group was heading in to another target now. He had to stop thinking.

"Overwork, this is Blackbeard, turn port thirty degrees on my mark. Ready, execute." The ships again leaned hard to starboard as the turning began. It was all so familiar now; they were back in the groove. The adrenaline pumped, the eyes opened wide, the nerves twitched with anticipation, and the voices fell silent. They had become conditioned. Responses were automatic now, they had become honed to deadly efficiency. Nothing compared to the degree of enlightenment or the intensity of the high they now felt.

Topside, the awareness of the gunners, the operations people on the bridge, the lookouts, and the spotters was tuned to a fevered pitch. Crashing waves of indigo water were sliced by four prows in close formation. The churning wakes of each of the steel giants foamed brightly as their propellers generated maximum thrust. There was a twinkling of starlight, a beacon here, the sound of a bell buoy there—it all melded into the scene as the Task Group bore down on the next target.

They made two more raids that night and, with the morning, were back in open waters again. In the blackness of the night the Task Group expended three hundred to four hundred artillery shells. About eighty were fired back at the flotilla, and on the beach there was a rash of explosions and fires and an unknown number of Vietnamese people died.

Ray had breakfast and hit his rack, tired and drained after a long night. He had been up most of the day before after only a few hours of sleep. He didn't know why, but he had awakened after only five hours of sleep the previous day. Later, he would come to realize it was the excitement of going back to North Vietnam that had charged him with so much energy.

Chapter 12

The Odds

On the evening of May 27 the strike raids continued once more. Between this time and June 4, when *Newport News* returned again to Military Region One, she fired another twenty-two missions against targets in the north, expending another 793 eight-inch shells and taking 188 more rounds of hostile fire, the latter to no effect. All but one of these raids were conducted under the same veil of darkness as the previous raids. The crew began to expect the night hours to bring combat, but they were learning just how one-sided these forays into the enemy's realm really were. The danger was distinct, there were continuous instances of hostile fire, and the excitement was both involuntary and regular, but the overflowing confidence of the young men was growing stronger with each venture.

On the 2nd of June the Task Group made a daylight raid against surface to air missile sites south of the Do Son Peninsula. This was the highlight of this period of action.

Early morning combat against North Vietnamese, June 1972

Five ships steamed to within eyesight of heavily guarded Vietnamese air defense systems in mid-morning and blew them away with impunity. The men were all elated. As the ships turned seaward and secured from General Quarters to rendezvous with the service ships, the weather decks became crowded with jubilant young sailors. They all basked in the sunshine and socialized with masculine, aggressive postures, tearing off their tee-shirts and striking muscle-man poses just as one might imagine a team of Roman gladiators returning victorious from the Coliseum.

Ray was walking aft toward the fantail where a large number of the crew was congregating in the morning sunshine, when Doc stepped from the mid-ship hatchway. Doc had a perceptible five o'clock shadow and rubbed his bloodshot eyes. He hailed his friend and took up stride with Ray.

"So what do you think killer?" Doc looked Ray squarely in the eye. Ray paused for a second not knowing for certain whether Doc was kidding. Then the mock serious look turned to a grin.

"I guess we gave 'em hell again," Ray replied. "And they were in it as well; those 130s were landing hot and heavy for a while, got pretty dicey for a few minutes."

"Oh yeah, it's not like they aren't trying. I guess we just keep 'em way too busy to effectively draw down on us, but I sure as hell wouldn't want to see what would happen if they hit us with a salvo of those motherfuckers."

"It'll never happen without the use of their fire control radars right? Isn't that what you told me? You of all people know that, right?" Ray surveyed Doc's face closely to see if he was feeling less confident than before.

"All it would take is one lucky shot in the right place, and we'd be history dude. How you gonna stop a 130mm artillery shell that's got your name on it?"

Ray hadn't really thought about it—it wasn't something any of them wanted to explore. *There's an element of denial about that*, he thought to himself. *Maybe it would be worthwhile to explore this dialogue a little further.*

"Well, what about all the armor this thing has on it? Hell, those 130s wouldn't penetrate six inches of steel."

"Look at the blueprints of this ship sometime," Doc said. "The armor you speak of is only in the critical places—around the magazines, the gun turrets, and the torpedo guard at the waterline; if they armored the whole ship the damn thing wouldn't float. Hell, from the main deck up the bulkheads and doors are only 3/8-inch sheet steel, those 130s would go through that stuff like cardboard. Same with the hull below the main deck, that's only one inch thick, an armor piercing shell would penetrate that too. You have to get all the way down to the waterline before you find the thicker stuff at the torpedo guard. That's sixteen or twenty feet of horizontal area from the bow to the stern that's vulnerable. What if one of those bullets, maybe even a salvo of them, just by chance gets fired right on the mark and takes out two or three frames of the Oh-One or Oh-Two level? Can you imagine three or four 300-pound bombs going off in our berthing compartments? Or in a fuel tank? Shit, this ship carries so much fuel and ordnance, it would go off like one of those munitions depots we've been targeting. I'm not trying to sound like a harbinger of doom, but if you think about it, we're putting ourselves in a pretty precarious position each time we go into one of these strikes. I really did not feel comfortable about this daylight raid at all!"

Suddenly the alarm bells were going off in Ray's head as he caught up with the scenarios Doc was proposing. *This really is a crapshoot at some level. Technology is a wonderful thing, but it's not infallible*, he thought.

"Well what do you think the odds are, Doc? You're a statistician, you're good with mathematics; what do you think the chances of them hitting us are?"

"Well, of course no one can say with any certainty what the actual math model looks like," Doc now took on a scholarly persona, "There are too many unknowns. You and I don't have enough information to calculate the odds with any accuracy." Doc paused stroking his chin. The two sailors stopped at the lifeline on the starboard side near turret number three. "But I have a gut feeling for the relative magnitude of the numbers, and I think if we made fifty of these strikes without someone in the Task Group taking a hit, it would be extremely unusual."

Ray thought about that for a second. "We've already done over twenty, and I don't see any signs of it slowing down. By all accounts this effort seems to be increasing in intensity. I think your calculations are askew, Doc. Sometimes we don't even get any counter battery from the beach. I think the gooks are holding back because they don't want to give their positions away and start taking our five-inchers in their faces."

"That may be true at times, but, from what I've read, the North Vietnamese are notoriously gutsy in combat, and I doubt they hold back much when they know taking us out would stop the horrendous pounding they are already taking. Many of those defensive gun positions are on our primary target lists anyway, so it's not like they're going to sit quiet and not worry about incoming."

"Good point. Dave's been telling me more and more about what he's gleaning from the strike plans and intelligence reports in Maincom. I guess they're pouring more coal on the fire in terms of gathering information. He said there are some SEAL teams working the beach, said there are some expected to be put on this ship soon, at least it's been discussed among the brass. His suspicion is they will be dropped off and retrieved in transit to and from our target areas to get first-hand Intel."

"That doesn't surprise me. It seems Charlie would be learning something from the experience and wanting to counter us any way he can. They might increase the defenses, throw more stuff at us, and try to come up with ways to gauge our positions better visually. Not that the gooks are all that brilliant, but remember, they've got Russia and China helping them. One of the articles I read in *Newsweek* said the North has some of the latest and most sophisticated Russian surface-to-air missile technology working for them, and it's getting pretty hard to keep the B-52s from being shot down. They're getting better at downing them."

"That's news to me! Not good news for us though, is it?"

"Well, I think that's one of the reasons we're doing all these strikes, to degrade the missile defenses the North Vietnamese are employing. The blockade of Haiphong and other North Vietnamese ports prevents them from receiving shipments in large quantities. There's more at stake here than what we see. It goes back to the old communism versus democracy Cold War thing. The Soviets and Chinese have a big stake in this and they're willing to lend all the support and technology it takes to keep us from winning the war."

"Well, that's been the belief I have held from the beginning, Doc. My uncle has talked to me about Cold War issues, and I have a great deal of respect for his views as a person who has been in on it from the perspective of a Colonel with the Strategic Air Command."

"Yeah, he would know. Well anyway, I think we're pushing pretty hard on the numbers, and I would not expect to keep doing this without some repercussions of a very negative kind. Think of the bombing campaigns over Europe in the Second World War, Ray. They finally put a limit on the number of missions a person had to fly before being shipped back home. That limit was twenty-five, and many of them, the majority, didn't make twenty-five missions without getting shot up at least to the point where they took casualties."

Ray looked out over the surface of the ocean. "Well, I'll think about that Doc. Right now I think I have to go hit my rack, I'm starting to feel punchy, need some sleep."

"OK, buddy, have a good rest. I'll see you later."

Ray ducked into the mess deck hatch and worked his way to the compartment. Back in his bunk, tucked snugly in and enjoying the cool of the air conditioning and darkness and quiet of the berthing compartment, Ray slipped off into dreamland. His last thoughts of the day centered on what Doc had brought to light; getting hit by the enemy really is a distinct possibility in this place. He thought a silent prayer to himself as he dozed off. *Dear God, please don't let us get hit by the enemy, keep us safe I pray. Amen.*

It was 4:30 p.m. when Ray became conscious of the real world around him again. The 1MC had just announced the securing of another refueling detail, and the ship was accelerating again.

The sounds wafted into his little sanctuary of darkness and warmth as he stirred and stretched, yawning. There were pattering feet on the tile decks, and the sound of aluminum lockers opening and closing as some of his fellows awoke and prepared their own waking rituals. Swanny was playing a guitar softly in the other corner of the compartment and humming the strains of "American Pie" while working out the chords. Ray looked at his watch and rolled on his side to face the metal barricade that separated him from RM2 Rodawald's bunk. As he headed to the showers, his thoughts drifted back to the conversation he had with Doc earlier.

He could see Doc's peering expression as he looked away toward the horizon in pensive contemplation. Ray recognized the seriousness with which Doc spoke. That moment, the bright sunny day with its blue sky and gentle breeze, a moment that had occurred just a few hours earlier, hung in his thoughts. *I think if we made fifty of these strikes without someone in the Task Group taking a hit, it would be extremely unusual.*

Taking a hit, incoming salvos, unarmored spaces on the ship; Ray began to put all of that into context. *Jesus!* he thought. *This is not a game, we're not impervious to their efforts. They are, have to be, trying their hardest to kill us; it's the only way they have of keeping us from killing them. And yes, by the way, we are killing them. The post strike messages, what did Dave call them? GDA, Gun Damage Assessment? They confirm that: Twenty here, unknown number of dead there, target destroyed, primary explosions, secondary fires, estimated enemy dead.* These terms all came flying back into his mind from conversations with Dave. He thought of Brian, lying in his casket—one day a strong, capable, handsome, young athlete and soldier, the next a cold, lifeless corpse. *Damn*, he thought to himself, *what insanity this is!*

The image of the B-52 raids again became vivid to him. *How can all that explosive force be unleashed in the confines of a city and not be killing and maiming hundreds, or maybe thousands, of innocent people? We're lobbing the same kind of destruction into Haiphong, the seaside ports, harbors, defensive artillery, and missile positions.*

He remembered seeing one message where a primary strike target was a group of naval barracks. His thoughts jumped swiftly back to memories of Norfolk and San Diego. He let his imagination run with the theme. Lying in his bunk at NTC San Diego in the middle of a dark night—then, with no warning, no precursor, no inkling of what was to come, the entire place turned to an all-encompassing torrent of fire, sound, and steel fragments ripping and tearing through everything as three or four 500-pound bombs arrived simultaneously. The horror, the terror, the helplessness one would experience, ever so briefly, before being pulverized into mush; or worse, being maimed and crippled for life or left to suffer for hours in an agonizing, pain-filled death.

Gooks wouldn't experience that any differently than we would, he thought. He was now becoming aware that it could quite possibly be the last thing he would ever experience in this life—fire, explosion, mutilation, suffocation, drowning. His imagination was taking off, he thought about the possibility of escape from that situation. *OK, one could conceivably be lucky enough not to get killed and, while the ship is going down, get off and start swimming.* Then he immediately remembered watching the sharks tear at garbage bags thrown off the fantail here in the South China Sea.

Now you've got the problem of making it to shore without getting eaten by sharks or bitten by sea snakes. And if that works out, you're safe. But wait, you're in North Vietnam, and you're the guy who's been bombing the hell out of these people and killing hundreds of them.

Ray thought about what utter helplessness one would feel, and the extreme fear and horror. For the first time he recognized his own mortality. He prayed again, this time a much more sincere and earnest prayer.

When Ray exited the mess decks through the after hatchway at 5:30, he had been up and about for one hour. Being freshly showered, shaved, and full of good food somewhat brightened his mood, but he still had pangs of anxiety. He had come upon a new reality. Doc had gotten him going on a disturbing thought train, and he needed to talk with others.

Don Foster was the first person he recognized as he stepped out into the late afternoon sunshine. Don was propped on a support post of the lifeline at the starboard side of the helo-landing pad. His lanky frame slumped slightly, and his arms hung heavily as though he was exhausted. His demeanor seemed calm; he was slow moving and somewhat lethargic. Don was a large man, just shy of twenty years old. He looked strong and rugged, with broad shoulders and muscular arms. One could easily picture him as a Marine or Army soldier. Don, at 6'0", stood taller than Ray who was only 5'9". Don was one of the Radio One crew as well, standing watches with Bird as his subordinate.

There were puffy clouds in the blue sky overhead and, looking forward, Ray could see a faint outline of land on the horizon. The salt air smelled fresh and clear, it was not particularly hot or humid. He was thinking to himself that this climate was not uncomfortable in early June, not at sea anyway.

"Hey Don, what's up?" he queried as he stepped toward his friend.

Leaning over the lifeline with a toothpick in his mouth, Don looked up casually with a glimmer of recognition in his eyes. "Oh, not much man. How are you doing today, just get up?"

"Yeah, I've been up for one hour or so, thinking about stuff and feeling a little antsy about something, can't quite figure it out."

"What seems to be the problem?"

"I don't know. I was talking to Doc this morning, and he got me thinking. He thinks we're cutting it pretty close with these raids, pushing our luck. He may have a point, what do you think?"

"Yeah, we're all thinking that way after this morning, I guess. They were getting pretty close to some of the other ships as we were coming out of the last one. The *OK City* got bracketed with shrapnel, and there was some damage to one of her launches. It seemed pretty gutsy to me to be going in during the daylight like that. What are they thinking, the gooks are blind? Eisenhower said they were gambling that we'd catch them by surprise as they were changing watches and feeling secure that the night was over. Guess it worked."

"Have you thought about what it would be like if we took some serious hits?"

"Nope, don't really want to think about that. Just hope Uncle Sam has our asses covered when it comes down to the nitty-gritty. My cousin was in the Army over here in '68. He says don't trust anybody to know what they're doing, calls it a cluster-fuck. Fucked-up-beyond-all-repair, FUBAR he says."

Ray and Don stood silently for a few moments. Ray observed the calm, matter-of-fact way in which Don communicated this notion, switching the toothpick from side to side with his tongue and glancing back and forth from the surface of the sea to the distant line of drab gray on the horizon.

Presently, Don took the object from his mouth and held it between his thumb and forefinger as he pointed toward the scene in the distance. "I know I wouldn't want to be on that piece of real estate, that's one damn thing for sure. At least out here you can get the hell away from it when the shit comes down on you. Those poor bastards are stuck there. When they start taking fire, all they can do is hunker down and wait."

"Yeah, I guess, but I've been thinking it could be pretty freakin' bad for us too if we took a serious hit."

"Like I said, I don't like to think about it." Don unceremoniously departed with those words, leaving Ray wondering if he had touched an open nerve.

As he walked forward, Ray took in the fresh air and late afternoon sunshine. The ship was heading west and slightly south now. *They must be going back to the south near MR1*, he thought. This gave him a feeling of relief, since the pace was less intense and things seemed more secure there. But it was strange that they were cruising in an unhurried way, within sight of the coast of North Vietnam. Looking out to sea he realized there were also two destroyers steaming their way at a leisurely pace several miles farther out to sea. He wondered what that meant.

It occurred to him that the emotional component of his experience had swung around from the jubilation of several days earlier to the relief that he was now feeling that the strikes were concluded for the time being.

Walking forward, he found Swanny talking with Larson and Bruce Woodings, two of the other antenna crew members of CR Division. D-Swan, D-Wood, and D-Larson were jocular and of bright spirit as they sat sipping coffee from Styrofoam cups and smoking cigarettes. They were sitting on the smooth teakwood main deck in the shadow of the outboard superstructure behind the starboard three-inch gun mount towers known as mounts thirty-two and thirty-four. Swanny's guitar sat across his lap, his massive size making it look more like a ukulele. The three were chuckling and exchanging banter. Ray had apparently just missed the punch line of one of Swanny's jokes; the big guy was adept at one-liners.

No one remembered who it was, but one of them had pointed out how gracefully RM3 Swanson moved around the various mast structures and antenna platforms strewn throughout the ship's upper rigging. It was quite unusual really, Swanny being quite rotund. The image was something like Jackie Gleason in *The Honeymooners* dancing around in a ballerina outfit. At any rate, one of them had referred to him as The Swan, and the name stuck. Through an evolution no one could quite define, it became D-Swan over time and then, once the naming convention had been established, the D became a prefix to all of the names of the antenna crewmembers.

The men greeted Ray as he approached, and they all exchanged a friendly round of salutations, some of which, in more sophisticated company, would probably have been considered crude, but this was the military style; "Asshole," "Dickhead," and "Motherfucker" were words of rapport to the young men of the crew. This again seemed some sort of expression of their toughness.

"Hey Swan, did you see the bunkers the Marines have set up on the tops of the towers aft of the bridge?" Larson was speaking.

"No, why, what are they?"

"Let's go look at 'em. I noticed them when I was up checking some long-wire antennas on the main mast. I'd like to check them out a little closer."

"Wanna come along Ray?" Swanny asked as the three rose from their seats. Swanny put the guitar in its case and tucked it inside the door as the four of them, coffees in hand, started up the ladder to the fourth deck level. Stepping from the superstructure onto the metal deck that was four floors above their previous position, they walked forward toward the rear of the flag bridge. Sandbags were piled neatly into a bunker-like structure twenty feet long and four feet high. These were formed into an arch, which ran fore and aft, its ends pointing inboard toward the centerline of the ship and the apex of the arch facing outward. Weapons were secured inside the bunker. A .50 caliber machine gun stood on a tripod, metal boxes were filled with belts of ammo, and another storage locker stood nearby marked "DANGER EXPLOSIVES." On top of the storage locker was a bazooka.

"Hey, that's a missile launcher," Swanny said. "Chief Yerks was telling me about that. The Marines have a shoulder-launched missile called Red-eye that is supposed to be able to shoot down aircraft. It has a heat-seeking tracking system of some type. They just installed this stuff because the old three-inch anti-aircraft mounts aren't fast enough to track fast moving MIGs. That's our air defense now."

The men all surveyed the equipment with awe. There were several other weapons lockers inboard and around the bunkers. It looked as though this would be a last stronghold if the ship were in close quarters with enemy forces.

"Damn!" Woodings exclaimed, "I hope no one is planning on getting close enough to use this stuff!"

"I hear ya dude," Ray responded.

The night was slow and causal on the watch in Radio One. Ray and Mike had a light schedule and took turns manning the operator's position and allowing each other time to take in the quiet evening in transit to Military Region One. Voice communications came in periodically from units on the beach and other ships, but for the most part things were subdued. The ships were proceeding slowly to watch the coastline for enemy surface craft or activity.

When morning came, Bird and Don relieved the watch. Ray and Mike went topside and walked the main deck back to the mess decks for breakfast. It had been the first time in four weeks that things had been quiet for twenty-four hours. There were no outgoing rounds and, more importantly, no incoming rounds

After a breakfast of powdered eggs, reconstituted milk, sausage, toast, and coffee, the two friends felt calm and content. They strolled the main deck for forty-five minutes and went down to Radio One, which in the daytime became a gathering place for members of the comm crew to get a cup of coffee and shoot the breeze.

Around 10:00 a.m. Ray and Mike returned to the berthing compartment for some sleep. Once again Ray lay back in the air-conditioned comfort of his bunk. The soothing quiet and darkness of the CR berthing compartment became a sanctuary as he drifted off to sleep thinking of the people back home; his Mom and Dad, sisters and older brother Art, and his nephews and nieces in Pennsylvania. *God it's so far away*, he thought. He said some silent prayers for their safety and asked his Creator not to let them experience another loss like Brian's death. Then he spent the last remaining minutes of his conscious moments thinking of Cynthia. She would be graduating high school in a couple of days, and he wouldn't be there with her. There was sadness, and there was love, and there was comfort here in his bunk. The war slipped away for a while.

Chapter 13

Heading for Liberty

In the late afternoon of June 3 the weather was warm and bright. Ray and Swanny walked about the main deck before dinner, basking in the sunshine and engaging in small talk as they observed the "Holiday Routine," as it was known in Navy jargon. It was like the leisurely cruises they had experienced in the Caribbean in previous years. The breeze was balmy, and the sea was bright blue and clear, almost effervescent where the bow wave separated the expanse of blue before them. There was no shoreline to be seen now, but on the horizon to the west one could make out two or three tiny puffs of dark smoke that told of the presence of some type of human activity, most likely warfare. Here, in the silence and warmth of the South China Sea, it seemed calm and placid.

Many of the other off-duty sailors and officers were lounging about the weather decks in tee-shirts and floppy sandals. Some wore cut off dungarees, others wore athletic shorts. The scene looked anything but military or regulation, a clue perhaps that the senior staff officers felt a little relaxation of the rules would be a welcome change.

"How long are we going to be out here Ray?" Swanny asked. "Have you heard anything lately about our schedule?"

"Not really Swan, it doesn't seem to be a very popular topic among our officers. Nobody's willing to venture a guess on that right now."

"Damn, it's been almost a month now since we left Subic. How long can we stay at sea?"

"The Chief says he thinks we can only fire the eight-inchers so many times before they have to be relined. He got that from the Weps officers. I guess the rifling in the barrels gets worn, and they have to replace the inserts with new ones so the guns maintain their accuracy. Dave says he's read messages that suggest they have to keep close track of the accuracy of the guns, because there are a lot of targets that are embedded in civilian populations, and they want to keep collateral casualties to a minimum to ward off as much negative press as possible."

"So that's what limits how long we can be out here. Hell, they get everything else shipped out here to us. If they can find a way to get the gun liners here we might not ever go back."

"Nah, word is it can't be done at sea; they have to use cranes and special heavy equipment in the yards to do that stuff. So we have to go back to Subic at some point."

Like most of the crew, Swanny and Ray were feeling like they were ready for some downtime. With the exception of two or three leisurely periods, the ship had been working a grueling, twenty-four-hour schedule for twenty-six days now.

The morning of June 4 found them in MR1 again, with no shortage of firing missions. They spent two days there supporting a South Vietnamese thrust into NVA-held territory north of Quang Tri.

On June 6 the ship headed back to North Vietnam and Operation Linebacker raids. It would be another ten days, and ten very busy nights, of coastal raids before *Newport News* would finally leave the war zone and head back to Subic on June 16.

Ray was walking aft on the port side of the main deck, happy the ship was on its way to the liberty port of Subic, when he noticed Dave walking toward him with a paper in his hand, which he appeared to be reading. He stepped into Dave's path and stopped five feet ahead of his approaching friend, realizing Dave had not looked up. When the out-of-focus image of a person suddenly appeared in Dave's peripheral vision, he stopped abruptly. A look of surprise came over his face, coupled simultaneously with a somewhat sheepish grin.

"Whoa," he said, "didn't see you there."

"If you'd look up from your reading occasionally, that wouldn't happen," Ray quipped.

"Yeah, yeah, bite my ass, I was reading something really interesting here. Look at this." Dave handed Ray the sheets he held in his hand.

Ray took the thermo-fax sheets Dave extended to him and began reading:

> 4June, *Newport News* returned to MR1 and TU 70.8.9. Action resumed as she fired five missions and more than nine hundred rounds at enemy targets. In causing four secondary explosions, she fired 874 eight-inch and thirty-one five-inch shells. One incident of hostile fire accounted for nine rounds.

> In the afternoon the ship rearmed from the *USS Nitro* (AE 23) at 1415. As in the previous day, *Newport News* fired in support of VNMC units. The ship operated in four missions and fired 260 eight-inch and 148 five-inch rounds, causing two large secondary explosions and starting one fire. At 1209 *Newport News* rearmed from the *USS Pyro* (AE 24) and then returned to the line….
>
> On June 6 *Newport News* steamed northward to rejoin TU 77.1.2 for *Linebacker* strikes on the coastal areas of North Viet Nam through the 16th of June. General Quarters was sounded at 2030 and thirty-six rounds of eight-inch were fired at various targets. GQ secured at 2238 at the completion of the mission. An early morning GQ (0130–0510 7JUN) began the *Newport News'* first day back north. Four missions were fired throughout the day, and 206 eight-inch rounds were fired.

"This is pretty interesting Bumbstead, where did you get it?"

"It's a copy of the official ship's deck log. It's the record of specific events, pretty cool huh?"

"This is amazing!" Ray continued to read the entirety of the ship's log, which covered the full duration of the ship's time in Vietnam thus far, before he headed off to dinner.

After a tasty meal of baked macaroni and cheese and fish sticks, Ray and Mike reported to Radio One to relieve Bird and Don at 6:45 p.m.. Even the mixed vegetables and dessert tasted much better than usual.

"Hey Ray, how was dinner?" Bird asked.

"Not bad dude, everything tastes better when you're headed for a liberty port."

"You know it buddy, and I'm hungry. Nothing to report, you got the watch, big dude. See you later."

By now the word was out that they were heading back to Subic and would be in port for a few days. The mood of the entire crew was upbeat and jocular, people were smiling, and greetings were cheery on the mess decks. There was a lot of laughing and joking during the evening meal.

It had been thirty-nine days since they left Subic for Vietnam. In that time, a great deal had changed in the lives of these young men. Most of them were really not all that aware of it yet, but the beginning of a significant metamorphosis had occurred.

Ray, sitting at the Radio One desk, reviewed the contents of the deck log Dave had shown him earlier. By now numerous copies were circulating around the CR division working spaces. It was truly awe-inspiring. The real time experiences of combat were only one perspective on the events surrounding the ship's combat activities. Seeing it all delineated verbally and summed up in numbers and terms that explained it further added another dimension to the experience.

The night passed slowly. Equipment and systems that had been up and functioning for nearly six weeks were now being shut down and deactivated so maintenance could be performed. The communications load of CR division suddenly fell off to a mere fraction of the pace it had been. The chattering teletype machines in Maincom fell silent with the exception of logistics traffic needed to get the ship into port. Most of the intelligence and tactical communications networks were secured. The voice radio circuits were silent.

Chief Yerks spent many hours in the Radio Chief's office putting together equipment maintenance schedules for the next week or so. The department Admin PO, Chief Pifo, was making up duty rosters and watch bills for the in-port period. By the looks, of it the forty-some-odd members of CR Division would be on liberty as much as possible while in Subic.

This is when it was good to be a communications radio person in the Navy. When the ship was moored to the pier, the communications watch could be shifted to NAVCOMSTA Subic, and there was no need for anything but a six or eight man maintenance crew to be present aboard until she departed again. This meant only two or three duty days, most of them four to six hours long for each person in CR Division. The rest of the time was theirs to spend as they pleased.

Ray was already calculating the amount he had saved in his payroll account. It was the first time in his life he had a bank account that numbered in the thousands. They had been at sea most of the time since leaving Norfolk in April. Now it was the middle of June, and for the last forty days they had been receiving combat duty pay. He felt, just a little, as though he was rich. Shipboard life was simple. If one did not play cards or gamble, the cost of living was limited to money needed for personal hygiene, cigarettes, candy bars, and cokes. When the ship was making ports of call on a regular basis, it was easy to spend your pay, but for the last three months their recreational expenses had been non-existent.

It was time to give some thought to using some of his windfall. Ray was thinking of Cynthia. They had talked about getting married when he came back to the States, or maybe after his separation from the Navy. If he chose to get out, it would be only another year and three months until his enlistment was up. Now might be a good time to get a diamond for his beloved.

In reality his nest egg was not all that great, but the buying power of $1,800 U.S. currency in the Orient in 1972 made it seem like much more.

The ETs had been communicating with some of their buddies in other duty stations in the Pacific who had been buying up Japanese and Korean made electronics, mostly in the audio technology realm. Ray had been talking with them and decided he would put a chunk of his wealth into a stereo component system. He and Swanny also tossed around the idea of looking for electric guitars and amplifiers in the Philippines.

And, of course, there would be plenty of pocket money for Subic, and perhaps a trip to Manila. Now that most of the stories of the Subic Bay "hospitality" opportunities had circulated about the ship regarding the first stop in the Philippines, the crew was very excited to return.

Ray felt a twinge of guilt when he contemplated finding pleasure with some yet-unknown Filipino lady-of-the-evening. But in his loneliness and desire for such comfort, he had decided the benefits would be worth the risk that Cynthia would ever learn of his intimate indiscretions. Risk had taken on a new meaning in the last few weeks. *There are risks, and there are risks*, he thought to himself as he sipped his coffee. *When your life is at risk on a daily basis, the other risks in life seem much less threatening. Besides*, he thought, *who knows if any of us will ever see the States again. We could all be dead next week. I need to get laid. I need to be close and intimate with someone, and I need to get really fucked up!*

This was not an uncommon theme among the crew. The steady grind, the twelve-hour days, the reality that death could at any point catch up with them—all these were beginning to wear on the consciousness of many. They all felt like conquerors, all young and brave and heroic, but there had been a glimmer of another reality.

I want a drink. I want a joint. I want to get fucked up! A good woman would make me feel a whole lot better. I want to wake up with a hangover and sleep in with a warm, soft, lovely woman next to me and know I don't have to be anywhere today. I just want some peace and quiet. Give me some solitude. Let me relax. Maybe I'll get really fucked up, go to sleep, wake up, and realize this was all just a bad dream.

They all had such thoughts as the ship slipped quietly through the inky black sea near the Philippine Islands. Some like Ray and

Swanny and Mike stood the watch in the quiet night while others dreamed in their racks.

Some of them, the officers and a few of the crew who came from families of wealth and influence, would have friends and family waiting for them in Subic. They would take leave and go to some exotic place where their personal relationships could flower in silence and peace and tropical beauty amid this otherwise chaotic part of the world. For most of the enlisted men, however, it would be what would seem like an eternity before they could touch and feel the realness of what they left behind. In the meantime, they would make an attempt to replace it with a facsimile.

After watch, Ray and Mike had breakfast and went out on the main deck for a smoke. The morning was hazy with patchy fog drifting on the calm surface of the sea. A dense humidity shrouded the ship, and her steel structures beaded with droplets of moisture as she steamed effortlessly through the sea. It was going to be a very hot day, though the temperature now was a reasonable seventy degrees.

Here and there, an island poked out of the mirror glaze of the inky indigo deep. The sun, veiled in gray, created a mere reddish-yellow tint on the eastern horizon. The drab, craggy, rock-like protrusions jutting from the smooth surface as the men scanned the panorama before them, suggested a field of black icebergs. The overall impression was one of an ominous, hellish place, devoid of life except for the existence of the 1,100 souls traveling though it. Ray thought of ancient mariners and what it must have seemed like to ply these waters in wooden ships before man had developed any real sense of our world in its entirety.

Newport News

Such a strange place, so quiet, yet so imposing; cold in visual presence in its grays, blacks, and puffs of fog, yet dense and hot like the inner regions of Hades. In some of his quieter moments Ray had been reading Homer's *Odyssey*, and it was not hard to envision the sirens calling to Odysseus from one of the dark spires. Was this a place of refuge or doom? These thoughts accompanied him as he made his way back to the compartment and the sanctity of his bunk.

He pulled the dark gray, wool blanket back just enough to allow the fluorescent lighting to illuminate his book and fished the volume out of its hiding place in the ditty bag which hung on the inside divider. He began to read another chapter in the epic tale of the mariner whose longing for his Ithaca was not unlike Ray's own desire to return to Norfolk, the States, Cynthia, his family, and sanity. Ray fell asleep, book in hand, dreaming of his return and the far-off love, security, and order of home.

Chapter 14

Loving Grace

At 4:15 p.m. the berthing compartment was still cool and dark, but not nearly so quiet. Ray stirred in his bunk. Rolling over on his stomach, he drew the forward corner of his makeshift blackout-curtain back and found the fluorescent lighting glowing brightly. Noticing the volume of Homer spread open on the floor next to him, he retrieved the book from its resting place and, searching for the book marker with his other hand, replaced it and stuffed *The Odyssey* back into the ditty bag.

From this perspective, just six inches above the shiny dark green floor tiles, he could see feet clad in flip-flops, white terrycloth shower togs, and the legs of many of his crewmates busily moving in and about the crowded spaces between the bright aluminum lockers and tiers of folding, aluminum-framed bunks. A few of the men wore utility uniforms while others were changing into civilian clothes, a dead giveaway that "Liberty Call" was about to begin. There were the smells of cologne, aftershave, and other toiletries drifting about. As the urgent movement of bodies around the premises stirred the air, a mixture of these smells came and went like the rhythm of waves gently lapping upon a sunny beach. Ray heard words of courtesy and annoyance as men moved urgently around the limited spaces.

The beginning of his day, whether a.m. or p.m., was always slow and arduous for Ray. Rubbing his eyes and stretching as far as possible in the limited space of his rack, he observed the scene further. Some of the feet were clad in sneakers instead of the usual military issue footwear. The denim jeans were bell-bottomed, and a few legs sported Bermuda shorts. Straining to look higher, he saw a few brightly colored t-shirts. *OK*, he thought to himself again rubbing the sleep from his eyes, *this isn't a dream*. Just at that moment the speakers of the 1MC crackled to life.

"Now hear this. Liberty call, liberty call. Liberty commences for all hands to expire in accordance with the plan of the day. Set the in-port watch detail. Now liberty call." The speakers fell silent, and he heard an audible, collective sigh of relief and anticipation. Men began exiting the compartment, raising their voices to communicate with buddies separated by the crowd in this confined area. Ray thought of cattle being herded into corals at auction, all the men attempting to queue up to exit through the same four-foot hatchway.

"Meet you on the pier Woody. Take your time, I'll wait for you."

"OK Swan, I'll be there ASAP."

"C'mon Dave, let's get moving."

"Don't get your balls in an uproar. It's gonna take fifteen minutes to get off the afterbrow anyway, relax."

"Yo Larson, I'll meet you at the EM club, I'm buying." The latter resulted in cheer from the entire crowd, followed by: "Everybody hear that? Jeffery's buying for everybody at the EM club."

And then, "Shut up Mac. I'm talking to Larson, not the whole department."

Happy would not have begun to describe the feelings these men were experiencing. Relief, excitement, euphoria, anticipation, joy, bliss, exaltation—all of these plus feelings of energetic glee were teeming in their collective mood of elation.

Within five minutes, the compartment was again back to normal with only a few sailors still sleeping or stirring. Ray lay back on his pillow and allowed his sleepy eyes to close once more and, as he did, he mouthed a silent prayer; *Thank you God for getting us back here safely.*

It took him another fifteen minutes to roll out onto the floor, grab his shower togs from the ditty bag, and snatch his towel from the frame of the bunk above his. He went to his locker and began spinning the combination lock dial automatically. In a few seconds he was opening the aluminum door and retrieving his toiletry bag. He turned quickly and followed the narrow passages between the bunks and lockers to the bright sunlight pouring through the hatchway at the forward end of the compartment.

Stepping into the mid-ship head, he found steam still evaporating from walls, and fixtures dripping with condensed moisture. The floors were wet and tracked with many footprints. Two or three of the twenty or so showers were still running in the room, which was as big as a locker room at the YMCA. So there were still some crewmembers aboard who, like Ray, were either on watch or asleep when the ship was moored to the pier and its gangplanks lowered. The mirrors and stainless steel sinks were smeared with toothpaste, shaving cream, and soapy water that had sloshed over the edges of the washbowls, and a few small puddles had gathered where the non-skid cement-like flooring was not perfectly level. All hands who were not either involved in the activities of mooring and securing the ship or sleeping off the mid-watch, had flocked to the head to get spruced up for liberty. This was a common event, but one which had not occurred for the crew of *Newport News* for the last forty days.

Ray took his time. He felt fortunate to have missed the rush; now he could calmly go about his waking rituals while coming to life again. He stuffed his gear into one of the showers and then exited the head and walked forward to the mid-ship "Gedunk," the refreshment stand that served the crew. The business window was shut with the "Closed" sign installed in place, but the coffee, soda, and snack vending machines were still operating. He plugged a quarter into the first of these and pushed the buttons to mix creamer and sugar into the drink and waited for the cup to fill before reaching in to retrieve it. It was machine coffee, strong and acrid, but hot and full of caffeine. Ray grimaced at the bitter taste of the hot liquid as he turned back toward the head to continue his leisurely routine.

Half an hour later, he was just finishing the task of shaving and getting ready to exit the head when Dave poked his head in.

"Hey dude, check this out!" Dave held a sparkling, new Canon F-1 camera in front of him and a shopping bag full of accessories in his other hand. "You won't believe the prices at the exchange—no tax, no import tariffs, nothing, rock bottom prices. I paid $135 for this. Get your butt going before they're all sold out, the crew is mobbing the place."

"Yeah, I'm about to go over there. Where are you headed?"

"Hurry up, I'll go back over with you. I want to check out the stereo gear."

"OK, give me a couple minutes to get dressed."

At the Subic Bay Naval Station's Base Exchange, there was a large number of the heavy cruiser's crew, but the store was huge and could have accommodated many more. It had been built and scaled up with the escalation of the Vietnam War and the overall growth of the Philippine support base. In 1972, it was much like the now common mega-stores.

They spent several hours there. Ray bought a camera and some lenses for it, a tripod, two tele-converters, an electronic strobe flash, and a carrying case for all of it. In the stereo department he purchased an entire component system of the best equipment on the market, with the advice of Doc and Herc, the ET/audiophiles. They had been boning up on equipment specs for weeks in anticipation of their own purchases.

By the time they were all done with their shopping, Ray and Dave had filled the trunk and back seat of a full sized Chevy cab to take their purchases back to the ship. Once they had everything aboard and stowed in what available space they could find around the many equipment rooms of CR Division, it was time for their second foray into Subic.

This time there was only one objective. They stopped at the NCO club for a couple of beers, because it was the closest bar on their way. Then they were off to Olongapo City, just outside the gate of the Navy base, where they began systematically working their way through the bars, clubs, and gambling halls. Within a couple of hours, they had become quite inebriated; none of them had had a drink in nearly one and a half months.

In addition, their thirst (not purely physical) had escalated with the level of stress that was collectively and cumulatively affecting them. Few of them realized that element, but it was certainly a factor in their behavior. Before six hours were up, the majority of the 1,100 sailors of the *Newport News* were in states of varying degrees of oblivion. Dave had returned to the ship after one and a half hours, but Ray, Bird, Swan, Larson, and Mac all met up in a second floor bar/brothel two blocks from the main gate of the base and settled there for the duration of the night. By 10:00 p.m. they were well on their way to an all-nighter. Of the twenty or so tables in the nicely appointed, air-conditioned, banquet hall style room, at least sixteen were occupied by *Newport News* sailors and the young women who had flocked to accommodate them. It was party time.

By midnight, Ray was beginning to reach his limit and felt it would be a good idea to find a room for the night. He and Grace, the lovely young Polynesian lady sitting on his lap, had already discussed the business arrangements and were hugging and kissing freely as they nursed the last drink of the evening. Singapore Slings, a spirited mixture of tropical juices and several liquors, were the going cocktail at their table. Grace had remained very lady-like, having only two or three all evening. The sailors, however, were used to taking their beverages in huge quantities, and despite the early effects in the afternoon, were now hitting their stride in the waning evening.

Ray sat back and looked at his lovely, young companion. Grace was very pretty, perhaps nineteen or twenty years old. She had soft, smooth, light-brown skin and beautiful, big, brown, almond-shaped eyes. Her cheekbones were high and slightly flared about a daintily proportioned nose. She smiled with full lips that were adorned with a deep red lip-gloss that perfectly matched the short, sheer, summer evening dress that gracefully covered her form. Grace stood perhaps 5'3", and he guessed her weight to be about 110 pounds. She was quite sexy, with elongated curves and full breasts. She smiled freely and her eyes twinkled as she glanced around the table with glee. And she was warm. She felt *so* soft and warm against his strong, young body.

"You butterfly ready to fly?" she said softly into his ear as she gently kissed at his cheek. "We go upstairs now?" She squeezed his hand softly and laid her cheek against his. "I take care of you now. We take long time to rest and make love."

Ray didn't need to be asked twice. He kissed her sweet face and took her hand gently in his, and they slipped stealthily into the shadows to the rear of the room.

At twenty years Ray thought, as most youthful lovers do, that he was a real stud. As he followed Grace up to the next floor in the twilight of the stairway, his eyes scanned her shapely form and the beautiful lines of her waist and hips. He marveled at the fullness of her smoothly contoured buttocks as they shifted beneath the light, Chiffon fabric of her fine attire. He wanted to be warm and gentle and loving with her he was thinking, go slow and easy, but as he was thinking passion was raging within him. He could feel the pressure in the front of his jeans as blood flooded into his genitals.

After closing the door with his free hand, he tugged gently on the dainty, soft flesh where their hands held one another and slowly turned her toward him. Ever so gently he moved closer and felt her warm breath on his cheek. His chest gently touched her firm breasts as they flowed into each other's embrace. He held her softly as though she was the petal of a rare and delicate flower, and breathed in a very long and gentle breath through his nose. The smell of her subtle cologne and mystique of her feminine pheromones soothed his nostrils and stimulated his arousal further. He kissed her soft, moist lips and felt the very tip of her tongue brush his own. Grace pulled him closer, in an increasingly measured gesture of desire as an almost imperceptible sigh flowed with the soft, warm air leaving her lungs.

"Oh baby," Ray whispered softly. He let his hands slide down slowly over her beautiful form, the narrowness of her waist and the smoothly outward sloping fullness of her hips, he began to become aware of the softness and creamy smoothness of her skin beneath the airy soft material of her dress. There was no panty line. His penis throbbed with the realization.

“Oh you heartbreaker butterfly,” she whispered, looking tenderly down into his expressive eyes. “You break many hearts, Joe”

Everybody in the military was Joe, short for GI Joe, here in Po-City. Her words were affectionate and soft as she slid downward raising her dress with her free hand and pulling it gently over her head. Then, shaking her long, silky, black hair free of the garment, she pressed her bare breasts once more to his warm face.

Chapter 15

Just Another GI Joe

The sounds of activity from the streets below rose up to the half-open, third floor window accompanied by tropical heat and humidity as Ray's awareness came into the moment. The bright sunlight streamed through the window, illuminating wisps of steam that drifted from the shower door. The strains of an unfamiliar Asian melody were emanating from the shower in soft, feminine tones as the cascading sound of splattering water was interrupted by the movement of Grace's soft form beneath the cleansing stream. The smell of lavender came to his consciousness as his darting eyes took in information about the beginning of this new day.

Ray reached for his cigarettes on the nightstand and lit one as he rose from the bed. The tiny room was already getting hot. *No air conditioning here*, he thought to himself as he glanced around reorienting himself with the features he had seen only in the dim lights a few hours before. He set the cigarette in the ashtray, stepped into the bathroom and slid the shower door to the side to expose his lovely partner. Grace's face was under the shower spray, her long black hair streamed down over her shoulder in silky smoothness. Reaching gently toward her, he placed his hand around her slender waist and stepped gently in next to her. Grace smiled; her eyes still closed to the rushing water, she touched his forearm and hand with intentional gentleness.

"Good morning, Joe," she said, "you sleep good? You snoring when I get up, I let you sleep."

"Good morning, Grace. My name is not Joe, I'm Ray, remember?"

"Sure, I know. How you feel Ray? You OK today? You hung over?"

"No, no, I feel fine, just a little dehydrated," he said as he opened his mouth to the cascade of lukewarm, chlorinated water and swished it around in his mouth before swallowing. He leaned over and kissed Grace's shoulder and softly hugged her body close to his. Grace slid the soap in her hand over his shoulders and began lathering his back as she responded in a warm embrace to his affections. The shower was refreshing and cleansing, and they played gently with the textures and contours of each other's forms for a few lingering moments, taking in the calm and the solitude of their seclusion.

"I have to go to work," Grace whispered in his ear as she softly kissed its lobe. "Must get going soon." She stepped from the shower and reached for the towel on its chrome hanger just an arm's length outside the shower door. The bathroom had just barely enough room for the two of them to stand without touching one another, a matter which neither of them found objectionable. Ray stepped out behind her and began blotting himself with the other towel. He tried to snuggle up once more to her naked form, but she stepped out into the bedroom gently pushing his hand back.

"Sorry honey, not now, have to go to work. I wait tables in the club. I hurry or be late, get fired."

"I understand," he said, "I'm just a horny guy I guess, can't get enough of you. You are a really beautiful young woman, Grace. Can we get together again tonight?"

"You come to club, I be there," was her response.

Ray fondled the burned-down cigarette butt sitting in the ashtray, his thoughts straying to the activities of the previous evening as he gazed at a long trail of ashes sitting in the bottom of the tray where the unattended smoke had been left. He dropped the butt, picked up the half-full pack, extracted another cigarette, lit it, and returned to a reclining position on the bed.

He watched Grace's soft, smooth, naked form moving about gracefully as she applied make-up, combed her hair, and patted the last of the droplets of moisture from her hair and shoulders. Then she slipped into her high-heeled, red leather shoes and retrieved the red dress from its resting place on the back of the room's solitary chair. She turned to the side giving him a final, profile view of her lovely, young body as she hoisted the dress over her head and let it float lightly over her form. With a wink and a smile, she darted daintily toward him, leaned over and kissed him lightly on the lips.

"See you later Joe, I mean Ray," she said, and turned for the door as she reached into her purse, pulled a lipstick out and began applying it to her supple lips. Grace strode briskly out of the room closing the door behind her.

Ray lay back on the bed, exhaling a puff of smoke and forming smoke rings as he let his mind return once again to the beautiful memories of their lovemaking. *Damn*, he thought, *she is incredible. I think I'm in love*. His thoughts were more in jest than seriousness, but he couldn't help feeling a closeness and warmth he had not felt since he had last seen Cynthia. At the same time, he felt a pang of guilt that bothered him. As he dressed and left the room, he contemplated the contradictory emotions that were playing tug of war with his conscience.

Ray stepped out into the hot, steamy street half an hour later, and, looking at his watch, noted the time. It was 11:40 a.m. and he had to be on watch in Radio One at noon.

The street was full of people bustling about, Filipinos hurrying here and there as they went about their tasks, preparing for another day of accommodating the Servicemen and furnishing their variety of trades in return for the money they could glean for their efforts. There were Servicemen in civilian clothing streaming into the off-base community and a smaller number, like Ray, making their way back toward the bridge over "Shit River" near the main gate of Subic Bay Naval Base. One could discern the general direction to travel back to the base simply by moving counter to the flow of GIs streaming into Olongapo City. Though it was only two or three blocks, the crowded buildings and people-filled streets obscured the military base from view.

Approaching the bridge, Ray recognized the main gate three hundred yards in the distance, its smartly-dressed Marine guards standing their watches, checking IDs, and saluting officers passing on foot or in black government cars or taxis.

The sky was blue with large, white, puffy clouds drifting overhead. Rickshaws pulled by motorbikes and Jeepny's (small vehicles made of parts from decades-old, discarded, U.S. government Jeeps) carried soldiers, sailors, and officers back and forth on the busy thoroughfare. The sounds were a mixture of beeping horns, jubilant cheers, and bursts of laughter as friends greeted each other while passing in the crowd.

Looking down from the bridge, Ray could see the brown, sewer-strewn, almost stagnant, water ten feet below. On both sides of the bridge, in the thirty-foot wide flow, were situated one dozen or so dugout canoes. Standing in each of these were one or two young, beautiful women (possibly adolescent girls or off-duty prostitutes) holding long-handled baskets and enticing the Servicemen passing over the bridge to toss coins to them. As the coins lofted through the air in their direction, each of these ladies showed their incredible poise and ballerina-like balance in retrieving the flying currency. None of them ever faltered, even when coins went long or wide of their position.

They simply let them go rather than reach outside their domain and jeopardize their precarious perches. The coins they did not retrieve fell into the dirty, brown water to be retrieved by their younger sisters and brothers swimming in the mire as they dove under and came up with the prize catch in their nimble hands. These were displayed with glee as the GIs cheered their efforts from the bridge.

Coin fishers and their boats in Subic Bay

Continuing toward the base, Ray made his way to the pier where *Newport News* was moored. He climbed the steps and crossed the gangway at the after-brow proceeding through the security station and on to the berthing compartment. Making a quick dash to the head to brush his teeth and shave, he returned to the compartment, changed into his utilities and reported to Radio One.

Chief Yerks and Mike were having coffee as Ray came through the hatch and turned toward the coffeepot with a grin in their direction.

"Hey, that's a pretty telling smile," Mike observed with a glowing grin. "Looks like someone got laid last night!"

Ray held his response in check and finished drawing his mug of coffee, stirring generous amounts of creamer and sugar into it. He turned and stepped back to the watch desk, grinning joyfully at Mike and the Chief.

"Well, how 'bout it Ray, find yourself a nice little Filipino mama last night?" the Chief queried with twinkling, blue eyes.

"Gee, I don't think she's a mama," Ray grinned.

"Yeah, I'll bet you got a pretty good look at her too," Mike chimed in, "all of her."

"Now come on you guys, you know it's not polite to talk about such things. My intimate relations with the opposite sex are my business."

"Yeah, long as it's the opposite sex they are," the Chief chimed in, "otherwise they're the Navy's business."

"OK, OK, that's enough," Ray grinned. He swallowed a swig of coffee. "You guys are real ball-busters this morning, give me a break. I just had a nice little interlude with a very lovely, young woman. I want to savor the moment for a bit."

Mike and Ray did some maintenance on the receivers in Radio One and Classified Control until 4:00 p.m., they then met again with the Chief, checked off their log sheets, and debriefed. Bird sauntered in munching on a cookie and relieved them of the watch, and Ray and Mike headed to the compartment where Dave and Kent were sitting at the table by the entry ladder. The four of them made plans to go to the NCO club on base and have a good steak dinner before going out on the town.

By 7:00 p.m. that evening, they had all enjoyed a thick steak with a salad of fresh greens and vegetables, a baked potato, two bottles of Matuse Rose, and strawberry cheesecake. The atmosphere was cool and lush in the air-conditioned dining room, and the relative quiet of this well-attended club made for casual conversation among the four friends as they exchanged information about their forays into Po City.

Ray began watching the time. By 7:30 he was feeling anxious. He wanted to make his way back to the club where he had met Grace, hoping to spend another evening with her.

It was the most relaxed and comforted any of them had felt in months, and they were reveling in the moment. As they drank after-dinner cocktails, the war in Vietnam seemed to slip away from their consciousness and they lost themselves in the simple pleasures of life.

It was 10:00 p.m. before Ray made his way back to the Green Garden Club. He looked around for several minutes before ordering a Singapore Sling. Seating himself in one corner where he had a panoramic view of the room, he sat back and listened to a young woman singing soft blues at the stage in the room's center. An ensemble of folk/rock musicians, all of Asian appearance, accompanied her. They seemed quite gifted as they ran through a medley of popular tunes from the era.

He watched for Grace for some time before noticing a couple entering through the darkened hallway at the rear of the room. It looked like Grace, but he could not quite tell for sure, so he moved a little closer. Gradually, moving closer still, he was able to confirm her identity. She was seated on the lap of a tall, handsome man who appeared to be a little older than he. Obviously an American GI, the guy was holding Grace's hand, but not paying particular attention to her. Ray waited until Grace was looking in his direction and attempted a slight wave to get her attention. It went unseen. After several minutes the opportunity presented itself again. Grace paused a moment looking in Ray's direction. Ray smiled, but still no response. After a few more moments Grace looked his way once more. Ray waved his arm a little more vigorously. Grace saw him and smiled in recognition.

There, Ray thought, *now she'll ditch this guy and come over here*. Several more minutes passed and Grace glanced his way once more. Ray motioned for her to come toward him. He could see Grace lean over to her male friend and say something. The man nodded to her, and she got up and walked to Ray. As she approached, her face took on a soft smile of recognition, and she extended her petite hand toward him. Ray took her hand and stood to kiss her on the cheek and said, "Hi sweetie. Can you come with me again tonight?"

"No, sorry Joe, I busy. Got date with old friend, not tonight."

"Oh Grace, are you sure? I thought we had something special last night. Don't you want to spend more time with me tonight?"

"Sure, I spend more time with you. Not tonight though, have date, have to stay with old friend tonight. You come earlier next time, I go with you. You come late I already have date, you know how it works, right Joe?"

"No, no, no, I told you, my name is Ray, not Joe. I'm not just another GI Joe. I thought we had something special."

"There lots of other girls here. I introduce you to my girlfriend, she take care of you. I see you another night. You know, we all butterflies, we go with other guys too. You meet my friend Jane, you'll like her. I go get Jane." She started to turn but Ray took her hand and pulled her back to him.

"No, wait Grace, you don't understand. I want to be with you. I like you a lot, and I think we could have something very special."

"No, look Joe, you wait your turn. I busy tonight, and I have date." She looked at him with apologetic eyes and forced a tender smile. "I must go now, my friend waiting. I can introduce you to Jane, she not with anyone tonight."

Ray's heart sank as he realized she was not going to give in to his request, but he had to try one more time. He pulled her closer and kissed her and whispered in her ear, "Please honey, I want only you. I really like you, I want to be with you. You know we're so good together, please come with me."

"I can't Ray, I have other customer. He already ask me, he my date tonight."

As Ray was about to speak he felt the looming presence of the tall, older man Grace had been sitting with.

"Do we have a problem here pal? I don't want to have any problems with you, but Judy is my date tonight. Judy is coming with me, you need to find yourself some other broad."

"Judy? This is Grace. We're friends, I'm just talking to her. I don't want any trouble either, I just needed to talk to her."

"Yeah, yeah, Judy, Grace, whatever. She's coming with me. You need to find yourself another whore, pal." With that he took her by the hand and led her back to the table they had previously been sitting at.

Ray stood there, his head reeling with disbelief and confusion. *Wait a minute*, he thought. *There's got to be a reasonable explanation for this. I know she has special feelings for me. She couldn't respond the way she did last night and just turn it off and then turn it on for someone else. Maybe she has me confused with someone else. Maybe she doesn't realize it was me—Ray from last night. Maybe she was really drunk and doesn't remember.* His mind kept going through the same iteration, trying to come up with some rationale for her behavior, and, as it did, he began to feel more and more like a dunce. First embarrassment, then shame, then humiliation filled his heart as he ran the gambit of negative emotions. The reality of it all settled in.

He picked up his drink and started to walk toward the door finishing the cocktail in three quick gulps. After several strides in that direction, a slightly taller beauty with high cheek bones and dark, curled hair tugged at his arm.

"Hi Joe, I'm Jane. How you doing?"

"Hi, not so well. I was just leaving."

"No, you stay, Grace told me to watch for you. We can go have good time. You go with Grace another time. I very, very good to you, you come with me?"

"No, no, that's OK Jane. I have to go back now, can't stay out, another time maybe."

Ray continued toward the door, and Jane tugged on his arm again. He turned abruptly and glared at her. "No Jane, not tonight, I have to go."

Ray made his way out the door and descended the stairway to the street. Stepping out into the hot, humid night he turned to walk back to the ship. His heart felt heavy and his mind reeled. *Jesus*, he thought to himself, *what the hell was I thinking?*

He had walked one and a half blocks through the crowded city street when he felt a strong pull at his arm.

"Ray, hey, you OK? Didn't you hear me calling you?"

Ray turned to see Rodney, one of the classified controllers from CR Division, looking him in the eyes and asking again if he was OK.

"Yeah, yeah, I'm sorry Rodney, I didn't hear you. I was off in another world. What's up?"

"Hey buddy, do you have twenty bucks I could borrow? I'm a little short. You should come and check out this casino, it's just like Las Vegas, come and check it out."

Ray followed Rodney for lack of desire to do anything else. He didn't feel like going back to the ship, and he certainly didn't care to look at another female. He didn't feel like doing much of anything. He was hurt, embarrassed, and depressed that what had been such a wonderful, unique encounter to him seemed like nothing to the other party involved, whatever her name was.

They entered a large building with an institutional looking concrete façade, much like a bank or government building. Inside they found a tunnel-like hallway with green velvet walls. Dark green floor tiles were buffed to a high sheen on the spotlessly clean floor. At the far end of the chamber was what appeared to be a huge vault door, as one would expect to see in the inner sanctum of a large Manhattan banking firm. As they approached, the door opened silently and effortlessly, despite its gargantuan proportions. Inside was a large, plush, green velvet-walled room. It was cool with ample air conditioning and had bright, indirect lighting, distributed to create alternating areas of brightness and shadows. Crystal chandeliers sparkled in the luxurious cavern. There were no windows, but tastefully appointed overstuffed chairs and sofas abounded, along with green velvet gaming tables, large roulette wheels, and rows of slot machines.

The customers all looked to be American Servicemen. The women were all Asian and, like the girls in the Green Garden, were very good looking and ranged in age from perhaps eighteen to twenty-five. Many of them wore evening attire and classy looking clothes. Some were dressed as dealers and waitresses in dark charcoal gray, three-piece suits. All had china doll painted faces and eye make-up that looked perfectly applied.

Ray and Rodney browsed around amid the semi-crowded interior of this soft, cool oasis of tranquility. Young men in civilian clothing with military haircuts sat or stood at tables all around the premises. Refreshment carts and tobacconist carts were being pushed from table to table by lovely, young women who had a smile and a soft touch for each of the customers. The two friends took a seat at the first

Blackjack table they came to, and Rodney placed a bet as Ray looked on.

A pretty, well-dressed woman strode to them and asked for their drink orders. Ray asked for a gin and tonic, Rodney ordered a bourbon and coke. A second lovely lady walked gracefully toward them with a cigarette tray. Ray reached out and took three Marlboros from the opened packs of American and British cigarettes. He reached into his pocket pulling out a roll of bills as the girl smiled sweetly and said, "No no, you gamble everything on the house. You no pay."

Damn, Ray thought, *that's very congenial of the house, free drinks and smokes, not bad.*

Just then, another very attractive, and quite shapely, Filipino girl walked up with a tray of freshly made finger sandwiches, as nicely presented and appetizing as any five-star hotel might have offered. Ray took a bone china plate and placed three of the small sandwiches and a pastry on it as the girl's twinkling eyes smiled pleasantly at him.

"Thank you," Ray managed.

"You're welcome," she said in perfect English, "my name is Edie. If there's anything I can do to make your visit more comfortable, don't hesitate to ask for it. I'm here to serve you." She smiled sweetly and breezed by as if floating on a cloud in the direction of another table.

Ray watched her walking away with perfect poise and grace. Her firm, round buttocks swayed effortlessly beneath the soft, black, perfectly tailored, silk skirt that clung to her shapely hips. *Probably another Grace/Judy or whoever*, he thought, *boy they sure have some really fine looking women here.* He broke his stare intentionally as the stinging feelings of loss and embarrassment returned in a wave of self-pity. *Jesus*, he thought, *what a duff I am to think I was something special to a very special woman. A fairy-tale love affair, a meaningful interlude; I was just another Joe to her, another fifteen-dollar date. I guess first come, first served is the way it really is. They don't care about any of us, they just want to pull as many tricks as they can and take our money.*

Still, there was something inside him that said there was some sort of meaning, some sort of gentleness about Grace. *She couldn't have just been in it for the money alone*, he thought. *She really enjoyed it, I know she did.* His confused mind started obsessing about her again.

A slap on the back from Rodney brought him back to the moment as the drink lady returned with two tall frosty glasses. Ray was ready for a few stiff drinks so he ordered two more each for himself and his friend as he reached for the gin and tonic and turned to face Rodney.

"Here's your twenty back bud," Rodney announced with glee as he flashed a roll of brand new twenties. "Black Jack and a natural pays triple, not bad for a three hand run is it? I made 120 bucks."

Ray's eyes lit up as he scanned the table. There were only three players, and the dealer looked so young and innocent, she couldn't have been any older than a teenager. He decided to try his hand. He took a long pull on the ice-cold gin and tonic and placed $2 on the table.

It was 3:45 a.m. when Rodney and Ray stumbled out of the casino. They had both done quite well by Po City standards. Rodney had over $500, and Ray was just shy of $200. They staggered and swayed back to the base and through the guard station where the two Marines on duty rolled their eyes and grinned at one another. Ray thought he heard one mumble something derogatory to the other, but couldn't quite make it out and thought better of challenging the obviously condescending manner of the grunts.

They looked every bit the quintessential drunken swabbies as they rocked back and forth and side to side climbing the steps to the after-brow of the ship.

Chapter 16

Breaking Down Barriers

Ray woke with a start when Jerry shook him at 11:45 a.m.

"Get up dude, Chief Yerks wants to see you in Radio One as soon as you can get there."

"All right, I'm up. Tell him I'm coming." Ray rolled out onto the deck and stood up quickly. Suddenly he slapped a hand over his mouth and ran for the ladder and hatch, sprinting toward the mid-ship head. He shot through the doorway and into the first stall as vomit spewed through his fingers and down his chin. Thrusting himself forward. He grabbed the toilet seat and yanked it up as the full force of his uncontrollable retching flew forward in a stream of projectile vomit toward the commode. He retched for several minutes hurling with every ounce of his being as wave after wave of nausea overcame him. He began to stand up, and tore off a long strip of toilet paper to wipe his spattered hands and face. Just as he turned to exit the stall, another wave of violent spasms gripped him. Ray fell to his knees placing his hand on the toilet bowl to steady himself as he moaned and retched with agony.

Eventually he was able to regain his composure. He stripped off his briefs, stepped into the shower and washed himself for fifteen minutes as waves of nausea flowed over him. Twice he started for the toilet stall again and then choked back the spasms to regain control.

Descending the steps into the compartment, dripping wet with shower water, he tracked wet footprints across the compartment floor as he made his way back to his rack. He toweled himself dry and lay down. Ray rolled over, and went back to sleep.

Some time later a hand reached in and shook his shoulder again. This time it was Chief Yerk's gentle shaking that brought him around again.

"You OK son?" the Chief's soft voice asked.

"Yeah I guess so Chief. I feel pretty bad, I'm really sick."

"Not to worry. Mike is going to take the watch. There's not much to be done, just a couple hours of calibration procedures on the R1051s. You get some rest, we can take care of things. Got a snoot full did ya? I know what it's like. We're pulling out day after tomorrow. Sleep it off and get one last good day of liberty, it'll be a while before we get the chance again."

"Thanks Chief," Ray managed, "I'm sorry I got so fucked up. I really appreciate you letting me off. I'm really sorry about this."

"No problem son, sleep it off and don't worry. See you around noon tomorrow, you can take the afternoon watch, there's nothing much to do anyway."

After the p.m. watch the following day, Ray went to the mess decks and had the first solid meal he had eaten since the night in the casino. He felt much better and returned to the compartment, changed into civvies and left the ship to go into Po City.

He couldn't stop thinking about Grace. He really felt that she was someone special and wanted to try once more to talk with her. He knew it wasn't really love, probably just an infatuation, but the beauty of that night was still haunting him.

She must've felt it too, he thought, *I don't think she can be that warm and loving one moment and that cold and business-like the next. I have to see her one more time, just to be sure.*

Again a wave of guilt welled up in him. Cynthia's beautiful face appeared in his mind. He felt the love and warmth of her embrace and remembered her scent. *God, how could I do this to Cynthia*? he thought, *I know I love her more than anything in the world. How could I feel love for someone else and be so much in love with her at the same time?*

When he climbed the stairs to the Green Garden and entered the dining room it was 7:30. He looked around and saw familiar scenes: GIs eating dinner, some with their Filipino honeys, some with their buddies. Sexy-looking scantily dressed girls floated about and soft acoustic guitar music was playing from the stage. He sat at the end of the bar and ordered a bottle of San Miguel from the pretty maiden serving there. Taking a sip, he recoiled from the bitter taste. Lighting a smoke, he nursed the beer and watched the activities about the room. He saw no women he recognized.

One hour or so later, after finishing the first San Miguel, he felt somewhat more inclined to continue. He ordered another and lit another cigarette, looking around the room for the twentieth time. His attention was drawn to the petite, young blues singer now starting into her repertoire as the stage musicians filled in around her one by one.

A gentle tap at his shoulder diverted his attention. He turned to meet the smiling eyes of Jane.

"May I sit down with you, Ray?" she asked in fairly fluid English.

"Sure, hi Jane, how are you? Is Grace here too?" He immediately realized how obsessed he sounded.

"No, Grace not here. She had to go home, back to Manila. She ask me to watch for you. She gave me note to give you." Jane held out her soft, smooth hand to reveal a folded sheet, reminiscent of a schoolgirl's study hall note slipped secretly to a budding love interest.

Ray took the paper and slowly unfolded it to read:

Dear Ray,

I am very sorry you are hurting for me. I want to see you, but I already had date that night. I think you are really good guy, I think we are good for each other. If I can see you again I will be your girl if you want me. I think you are beautiful lover and very handsome man. I don't want to hurt you, I love you very much. I have to go to Manila to take care of my mother, she very sick. I don't know when I can come back to Olongapo City. I want to come back as soon as I can. I hope you will be there again and we can be together. I really very sorry if you hurt, I want to make it up to you. Please do not hate me. Please remember the night we spend together. I will never forget it.

I love you,
Grace

Tears welled up in Ray's eyes as he re-folded the paper. Jane stood a few feet away, looking in another direction. She glanced back at him as he stuffed the letter into the pocket of his jeans. His chest heaved. He let out a long sigh and wiped the tears from his eyes and cheeks. He turned away from Jane and lowered his head as he lit another smoke.

Jane approached and placed her soft hand on his shoulder. Ray turned slowly, the cigarette shaking in his trembling lips.

"I sorry Ray. I know you really hurt for Grace, and she hurting for you too. She told me she really love you a lot. She ask me to give you letter and say she hopes to see you again. You want to step out on the balcony with me and talk for a while? I will stay with you for a while if you want me to." She paused, "I know you hurting honey."

They walked up a flight of stairs, out into the hot evening breeze, and sat at a table on the balcony on top of the roof of the Green Garden. The stars were glowing faintly through the humid air and the ambient light of the city. The salt air wafted in wisps, and Ray smelled the sea breeze flowing in from the harbor. They sat together and talked a little. Jane told him that Grace was her best friend. They had come down to Po City together from Manila to make money for their families, and Grace's mother was very sick with cancer and was not expected to live. Grace was the oldest of five children. Her father had died two years ago when Grace's youngest brother was five. Now her mother was dying, and she would have to take care of her sisters and brother and get things settled in Manila before she could return again.

"I'm sorry Ray, but I don't think Grace will come back here. It will be too hard for her sisters and brother, and she does not want them to come to Po City and become prostitutes and beggars like most of us here."

They sat together for a while before Jane pulled something from her purse. It was a joint. She held it to the light and tore off one of its tightly twisted ends to open it for smoking.

"Do you want some of this? I don't know if you get high, but I like to smoke it sometimes."

"Sure, I could use a little buzz I guess. I wish I could have talked to Grace before she left. I wish I had come back here and talked to her."

She lit the end of the joint and took a long drag on it, handing it to Ray as she held the smoke in for effect. Ray reached for the smoke, held it to his lips, and, doing the same, took a long toke on it.

"I don't think it would have helped to talk to her," she said, exhaling the smoke as she talked. "It would only make it harder for her to go back to Manila. She hurting very much for her mother, and she hurting very much for you too. It would have been harder for her to leave if she saw you again. She really like you a lot, she want to be with you long time. But you have to go away again, back to Vietnam, and she would not know if you come back or if she ever see you again. She had to go back to Manila. I don't think she will come back here."

They smoked and talked and provided company for each other on the balcony. The pot was good, and the drinks went down easier and easier as the waitresses brought them repeatedly. Ray had switched to Singapore Slings, and the combination of those and the marijuana took him to a wonderfully lofty place where comfort seemed much more important than anything else. Jane leaned toward him and smiled softly, her almond eyes both twinkling and empathetic. Ray placed his hand on her cheek and gently summoned her waiting lips closer to his and they kissed.

Jane smelled wonderful. Her light, airy perfume, a subtle intoxicant, added to the warm and comfortable alcohol and marijuana buzz in Ray's head. They kissed again, more passionately, yet still very gently as she slid her long slender fingers and forearm around his neck. They were both feeling warm and fuzzy inside and the stars had gotten brighter as the night darkened. In a few more minutes they were embracing softly and warmly, ever so slightly increasing the pace of their affections toward each other.

Jane sat back and looked at Ray with longing eyes. "Oh boy, Grace is right. You are wonderful man. I like being with you, how long you be here in Po City?"

"We're leaving tomorrow. We'll probably be back in another month or two."

"You kill VC in Vietnam?"

Ray looked down at the floor and thought for a minute. "I don't personally kill people. I work with many others, and we kill VC together. It's what we have to do. We are at war with them. I don't hate them really; I don't really know anything about them. I just do what I have to do."

"I know, I know, war not your fault, you just soldier, you have to do it, I understand. Viet Cong bad, Viet Cong kill many innocent women and children, torture many people. They animals, they kill for fun."

"I don't know if that's true, I just hear reports about them. I've never even seen them, just the films of the damage and disaster they cause and we cause. It's all fucked up. It's really a mess. I hate the fucking war. What is wrong with these people that they have to kill and kill and kill one another?"

It was the first time Ray had ever realized this emotion. Here on the balcony patio of the Green Garden Lounge in Olongapo City, Philippines, in the presence of this beautiful young woman, he was finally coming to grips with the mass chaos of war and all its craziness and horror.

"I just want to go home," he blurted out, "I just want to go back to Pennsylvania. I don't want to kill anybody. I don't want to get killed or see any of my buddies get killed." He started breaking down and wept openly for the first time in his adult life. He felt pain. He hurt. Suddenly he was ashamed and wanted to leave. Tears streamed down his cheeks, and he was embarrassed. What would Jane think? How could he face her? He wanted to disappear.

Jane leaned forward and cradled him in her arms. She drew him to her breasts and she sighed. “It’s OK honey, you are good guy. You don’t have to hurt for them. The VC are evil, mean, horrible animals. I think you just trying to stop them from killing many innocent Vietnam people. It’s OK, honey. It’s OK. You cry, then you feel better.”

The night seemed far too short even though Ray had no inclination to sleep. They lay together in a loving embrace for hours and hours. They made love slowly, tenderly, and so very gently, touching and holding and comforting each other all through the night. They cried together and wiped the tears from each other’s eyes. They kissed each other’s bodies in all the most private and tender places. Ray and Jane bonded—a young, strong, American Serviceman in tears and a soft, smooth, alabaster, Asian female with beautiful, big, brown eyes and soft, jet black, flowing hair; her heart hurting for him, for her best friend Grace, and for herself. She feared she would never see him again.

Chapter 17

Facing Reality, No End in Sight

Schedules being how they are, *Newport News* was not to leave Subic for another three days. During that time Ray and Jane spent every evening together. She made sure not to make other "dates," and they enjoyed each other to the fullest.

On June 25 the ship left the pier at the Naval station and headed out into the harbor to return once again to Vietnam. The afternoon was dark and cloudy. A brisk, yet hot sea breeze was blowing white caps on the surface of the gray sea as the ship accelerated past the dark islets scattered here and there at the mouth of Subic Bay Harbor.

Ray stood on the fore deck having his after dinner smoke and trying, with little success, to keep from thinking. He saw the images of his two Filipino lovers, their beauty invoking pangs of emotion ranging from sorrow and loss to love and comfort. As soon as he focused on these, the haunting image of his beautiful Cynthia overtook him, and his heart ached with guilt and agony at the thought of betraying her trust. *How could I have done that?* he thought. *I love her so very much, and she is so wonderfully and lovingly devoted to me.*

Just as these thoughts humbled him, the ominous weather forebode their impending return to the war zone. *Will I ever see any of them again? Will we ever come back here? God, I'm going crazy, I can't think about this anymore.* But he could not stop himself from thinking about any of it. He was a tangled mass of emotions, and on top of that, he felt foggy and queasy from the aftereffects of the previous night's debauchery.

The ship's speed increased, and the wind blowing over the bow became greater and greater. His hair blew back and the cigarette glowed brightly as he puffed the last few puffs, facing the oncoming storm. There was an empty feeling in his stomach which he could not identify. *Was it nausea? No, not really. Was it heartache? Sorrow? Fear?* The feeling was more intense than anything he had felt, but still he couldn't identify it. He remembered what he had told Jane, "I hate this fucking war!"

On the 26th, after steaming at flank speed once again, the crew found themselves firing gunfire support missions in support of ground troops in the quagmire that Military Region One had become in Quang Tri Province. A battle was raging between the tenacious North Vietnamese and the more tenuous South Vietnamese Army and Marines, who hung on only because of the tremendous support they received from U.S. Forces in the air and along the shorelines. Quang Tri City, the provincial capital, had been totally reduced to rubble. B-52 bombings and naval gunfire had destroyed every standing structure and pummeled the existing mounds where buildings had once stood to create a landscape of broken concrete, bent steel, and shards of glass. The news clips circulating around the fleet, off the coast, continued to generate new highs of shock and disbelief among the sailors and Marines.

Because the thrust was to hold ground against the new onslaught from the north, *Newport News* participated in only one Linebacker raid in the north between June 26 and August 3. There were the occasional instances of sparsely scattered incoming artillery as one or another of the ships ventured in close to shore to reach farther inland with their guns, but harrowing moments were few and far between. The Seventh Fleet units in MR1 experienced no major damage. The schedule was nonetheless busy, and the twelve-hour days stretched on and on, interspersed with refueling, rearming, and replenishing the ships' consumables.

On July 27 the ship incurred its first combat damage in her twenty-four year history. While loitering one mile from shore to allow her eight- and five-inchers the reach required of their mission, a lone 130mm artillery shell exploded just yards from a five-inch fire control Radar on the starboard side aft superstructure. Shrapnel from the burst shattered the windows in the unit and perforated its metal housing and two-meter dish antenna, rendering it useless. The director was not occupied at the time and no one was injured. The blast sent one dozen or so startled sailors, previously lounging about the main deck, running for cover and screeching with excited expletives. The experience was a reminder that death was never far away.

Ray's job in Radio One had become, at times, very interesting while at other times very mundane. He and Mike were standing the day watches now and voice radio traffic was constant between the ship, other units of the fleet, spotters, and ground forces on the beach.

The one foray up north entailed a single raid on a SAM site several miles inland near the Don So Peninsula. The raid occurred at 2:00 a.m. and, by this time, Ray and the rest of the crew had become so accustomed to hearing the guns fire all day long that few of them even stirred in their sleep when the fusillade of artillery left the ship. Ray's sleep was only slightly interrupted, enough for him to almost consciously realize the ship was listing suddenly and firing rapidly. He turned over and re-entered his deep relaxing doze. Though it seemed like ages since they had left Subic, August 3 brought the news that they were once again headed back for a few days of maintenance and R&R. The crew was jubilant; they had dodged the bullet once more. Perhaps this was the way it would be for the rest of their time in Vietnam. If so, most of them felt buoyed by the prospect. This was not really too much to handle. Maybe it was getting better.

The sailors had another package of images to add to their experience in the form of constant palls of smoke rising from the lush jungles, flashes of artillery coming from the coastal highlands in the dark night, Huey Cobras and F-4 Phantoms bearing down on tenaciously held positions in the day and unleashing their furious barrages of offensive might at the enemy. The dull thuds of explosive ordinance in the distance and popping of heavy machine guns were discernable at times to crewmembers on the main deck and weather decks topside. There were many excited radio calls from soldiers under attack by massive numbers of enemy soldiers who came in waves unexpectedly, both in the night and in the day.

Sometimes Ray heard excited spotters calling for immediate salvos from the ships and planes to help stave off enemy assaults. Sometimes he heard excited calls for "medivac helos" to extract the wounded or dead. Sometimes the radio fell silent never to respond again. Ray knew these were "friendlys" who had either had equipment failures or had been killed.

All hell was breaking loose back in the States as well. The news clips from home were carefully edited by AFRTS to exclude the most damaging and demoralizing stories. Letters from home and the wire service reports brought story after story of demonstrations on college campuses, the gates of military bases, and city streets back in "the world." World news was dominated by statements from the Russians, Chinese, and Koreans as well as other nations that opposed the resurgence of military action in Southeast Asia.

The party line of U.S. politics was that U.S. forces continued to be withdrawn from Vietnam and casualties were declining. These statements intentionally neglected the increasing fleet strength and air assets of the U.S. military machine. The real picture was skewed in favor of the number of "in-country" personnel being shipped back home.

Ray began to understand how numbers could be manipulated to reflect what the government wanted people to perceive. Even the casualty numbers were altered. "Vietnam casualties" were considered only those who were killed in-country, and the small numbers they reflected were only American military personnel. The South and North Vietnamese killed in this latest clash were overlooked. It wasn't in the interest of the war to list the losses of our Asian "friends," and the government had long since realized that running body counts of enemy dead had a negative effect. The fact was that the North Vietnamese were being decimated in large numbers, and this was not a popular image to present to the world.

If soldiers, sailors, and airmen were evacuated to nearby countries or hospital ships and died later of their injuries, they were not counted as "Vietnam combat casualties." *An interesting twist*, Ray thought. *If a SEAL team member, riverine patrol grunt, or airman gets hit, is evacuated, and dies on a hospital ship in international waters or a hospital bed in Guam, Thailand, or Hawaii, that death does not get reported on the list of Vietnam casualties. Pretty slick.* His thoughts were cynical and sarcastic. He felt guilty and trapped—he had signed the security clearance agreement that bound him to silence. Was he complicit in these lies?

But now they were headed back to Subic, and he would again see Jane, and perhaps even Grace. The issue with Cynthia had been somewhat resolved. In their almost daily letter writing, Ray and Cynthia had come to an understanding. After long deliberation and careful thought, he had decided to make a request of her. While expressing his fondest devotion and honest love for her, he had managed to discuss, quite artfully, the facts of his life in the war zone in terms that sounded reasonable and, at the same time, not too shocking. The letter started out:

> *My dearest love,*
>
> *Don't ever feel I do not constantly keep you in my thoughts and dreams. My love for you can only grow with each moment we are apart. For me my dear, I can never imagine not loving you forever, and I will always be devoted to your beautiful love for me. But I have learned new things about life and death here in Vietnam, and it is with these new perspectives in mind that I feel I must express these views....*

It explained that he knew they both had to accept the possibility of his tenuous mortality in a war zone, that it was futile to ignore the possibility they would never see each other again, and that he felt they both had to do whatever was necessary to accommodate that reality. The letter went on to gently address his and her needs for comfort and solace. He gave her his warmest love and asked her to forgive his ideas if she could not understand his motive, but he felt they should put their relationship on hold until he returned, if that was agreeable with her. They would still communicate and proceed toward future plans, but allow the freedom for each of them to have the "experiences they might need" to get through this terrible period of separation and uncertainty.

It's a polite way of saying, I need to live while I have life to experience, he thought to himself as he licked the envelope and stamped the letter, a tear in his eye. *I pray she does not hate me when she reads this.*

There was a ten day break in her letters before he received a response from her, and he knew what that meant; he had hurt her terribly with the thought that he would betray her love for his own needs. But when the letter finally came, she had gotten through the initial reaction and thought it through before responding, as steady and understanding as she had always been in their relationship.

My dearest, darling Ray,

I will always love you more than life itself, regardless of what you choose or who you choose to do it with. I understand, more than you could know, how you feel. Knowing what Mary Pat went through with Brian's death and how you also have been affected by it, I understand how you must feel. I've talked with my Priest about it, and he has helped me greatly to understand and forgive your decision. Father John was a chaplain in Korea and tells me it is nearly impossible for soldiers and sailors not to take what they can from every opportunity to experience warmth and affection after long weeks of combat. I can't say it doesn't hurt me to think of you in someone else's arms, but at the same time, when I think of Brian, all alone in Vietnam, without anyone to turn to when he needed, I pray he had a lover to comfort him in his last days.

I am crying as I write this, but I have to remember what Father told me, 'If you love something you have to let it be free. If it returns to you it is truly yours, if not, it never was.' Please be safe and come back to me. I will welcome you with open arms.

Love always,
Cynthia

For several days after receiving it Ray felt horrible. He felt he had just turned away the most wonderful, beautiful thing he had ever known, and he feared she might try, and even worse succeed, in putting his painful memory out of her life completely. *Maybe it's better that way*, he told himself. *I couldn't bear to devastate her the way Mary Pat was crushed by Brian's death. Please Lord*, he prayed, *let our love survive this time in hell.*

* * *

The Green Garden was exactly as he had left it when he half ran through the door. He looked excitedly around at the tables filled with men and women. It seemed to be the very same crowd as the day he had left. The stage was alight with a five-piece rock band blaring out Big Brother tunes. A young, Asian version of Janice Joplin belted perfectly-covered vocals of "Piece of my Heart" from behind what seemed to be a huge bottle of Jack Daniels. She slugged the bourbon like water between assaults on the microphone as she imitated the stage presence of the now-dead singer.

"Shit!" Ray exclaimed aloud, "they're great!" If they weren't Filipinos he would almost have believed the resurrection of Janice herself had taken place. He looked around again for a familiar face. There were probably two hundred people in the room. He fought his way toward the mob surrounding the show at the center of the room to get to the other side. He strode purposefully around to each corner, looking in all the dark places; he stopped and rubbed his chin.

OK, wait a minute. First of all we've been gone for forty-five days. Second, she has no way of knowing I'm back. Third, if it's business as usual, she may well be upstairs with somebody else. Calm down, calm down. Then he thought for a moment. *Which one was he even looking for—Grace or Jane?*

He bellied up to the bar through a crowd of thirsty young men and held up a five-dollar bill. One of the busy bar tenders glanced his way and he yelled, "Gin and tonic." The drink was whisked to him almost immediately, and the five disappeared from his outstretched hand. A moment later, four ones appeared back in his palm. He yelled at the male bartender already taking another drink order. "Is Jane around? How 'bout Grace?"

"No Jane, no Grace, I just make drinks. You find girls yourself." Ray turned and looked for a familiar face.

By the end of the second day in port he had visited the Green Garden four more times and talked to nearly every prostitute and waiter in the place. No one knew of Grace or Jane. Only one person even responded to the names. "Jane leave here," she said, "work someplace else now. I not see her in many weeks. Don't know any more, you want to be my boyfriend? I think you pretty nice. I good lover, show you good time, long time. Very cheap, special deal for you, Joe." She hung on his arm as he continued to look around.

OK, he thought to himself, *so that's how it is. I get it now. These ladies come and go every day. Here today, gone tomorrow. All right, I can handle that, I guess. So it's just a matter of who looks the best to me. 'My pleasure' as they say. Here we go.*

In the morning, Ray and his new partner talked a while before they left the room. After hearing Ray's version of the story of Grace and Jane, Olivia spoke, "They knew it was your first time in Subic, you cherry. They be very gentle with you, make you think they honest girls. Have hard luck story to make you feel sorry, maybe get you to marry them. It all bullshit Joe. Filipino girl want two things from GI, money or ticket back to USA—sometimes both."

Olivia, or whatever her name really was, was truly a veteran, a little older and not quite so subtle as Grace and Jane, but of the same ilk and profession. Olivia was a real pro; she had lots of experience, and it showed.

"Olivia know how to make GI feel real good," was what she said, and Olivia was *no* bullshitter. "Next time you go with Filipino Girl, you say I love you honey—no shit. Then they know you not cherry. They not try to bullshit you."

With mentors like Olivia to help him, Ray felt he could now find his way around Po City. The brief stay in Subic was much better this time. Again it was extended because of torrential monsoon rains that held up much of the work required to reline the guns.

Ray had changed. He didn't feel a loss or guilt about sampling the wares the young, female Filipino population had to offer. No strings, no pain, no sorrow, no shit. It was OK. In fact it was more than OK, it was enjoyable and fun. These sweet young ladies were loving, fun, and exciting, and they didn't require much of their GI friends other than a few drinks, a few bucks, and a little leeway to fly around and make themselves available to the next flower along their migration route. Like the migrating Monarchs Ray had known from childhood, these Asian butterflies were attractive, plentiful, and free. He had sampled three beautiful young women in as many nights, and had excellent and pleasurable experiences with each. The therapy this activity provided, in terms of lessening the stresses of warfare and opening his senses to escape its reality, were welcome indeed. He found himself in much better shape than when last they had left Subic.

Now it was back to the drudgery of MR1. He would be back on night watches, and sometimes he liked viewing the battle from a relatively safe position. The star shells (white phosphorous flares suspended from tiny parachutes to illuminate an area) reminded him of fireworks, and the explosions of bombs and shells were much less threatening at a distance. He was beginning to believe he would make it back home again.

"It'll be four months in a couple of weeks. They said this would be a six-month deployment, I might be home for my birthday in September." The world seemed a better place now, even with all the negatives of the war. He felt safer, more controlled, more confident, and, most of all, totally sexually satisfied.

The euphoria he was feeling changed about two hours out of port when the captain came over the 1MC for the first time in a few weeks: "This is the captain speaking. After a much deserved respite, I want to say first of all, I hope you all enjoyed the R&R. I'm getting many good reports coming back that seem to suggest most of you have found a home away from home and are having some good times in Subic. This is good, because we don't know exactly how long we will be here in WestPac. Seventh Fleet staff is quite impressed with our performance and has been thinking our contributions to the war effort are significant enough that they'd like to see us stay over here a little longer. No official word on that, but I've been instructed to let you know that there is a possibility our deployment may be extended a few weeks or months from the original six-month schedule. I'm sure some of you will not welcome that news, I myself am not particularly joyous about it, but we have a job to do, and our country and our loved ones are counting on us to do it.

"One of the reasons we are considering this change is that intelligence reports are showing another mass buildup of the Viet Cong and North Vietnamese regular Army staging in the north. It is fully expected that the Communists are gearing up to make another push to the south. For that reason, we're again being dispatched to Task Group 77.1 for resumed Linebacker strikes along the coast near the Hon La Island area. Some of these will be combined Air Force and Navy aircraft and surface ship raids, and it's likely some of them will get a little hairy. Because of the monsoons and the limited visibility, it may be necessary to make some of these strikes in the daytime.

"What I'm saying, I guess, is get ready for another rough ride. We expect heavy enemy resistance at times, so we're going to need to pull together and get back into our most efficient fighting mode. I don't need to tell you, but I want to remind you once again, I think you guys are wonderful. I wouldn't want to be doing this with any other crew than you people who are with me right now. So keep your peckers up and we'll all get through this thing together as one lean mean fighting machine. That is all."

Silence fell over the entire crew. For a few minutes there was no response at all. Then faint mumbles began to be heard. "Motherfucker," one said. "Son-of-a-bitch," came from the back of the compartment, simultaneously with the sharp thud of a fist hitting an aluminum locker. Then a rising din of angry voices began to chime in. As this all rose to a peak, a forceful and pointed voice rose above the chatter.

"OK, OK, simmer down. You heard what the captain said—we're all together on this team and we're going to pull together and make the best of it. We're some awesome, bad-assed motherfuckers, and we're going to get our shit all in one sock and march right up and punch Charlie right in the face. There's nothing to be afraid of and no reason to get pissed off. We had a pretty easy time of it last time out. This time it's our turn in the barrel again."

The voice was coming from Lt. Eisenhower who had been standing just out of sight behind the mid-ship passageway to the starboard side berthing compartment while the captain had spoken. All of the division officers around the ship were making similar statements to their subordinates. It had all been prearranged, and it worked. Within a few minutes, the men began to slap one another on the back and posture in their meanest and most threatening war faces, spewing forth statements of invincibility and resolve. When the Lieutenant turned to exit the compartment, he was smiling.

"That's the spirit men, keep your peckers up!" He echoed the captain's words and departed up the steps.

Chapter 18

Overcome and Numb

At 6:45 a.m. on August 17, the fireworks began again. For three hours and fifteen minutes, Task Group 77.1.2, with *Newport News* in the lead position, shelled and exchanged fire with enemy coastal defense and surface-to-air missile sites once more. The counter battery was light to moderate as the three cruisers of the group expended around 1,000 rounds of artillery, causing numerous fires, explosions, and casualties. Adrenaline pumped through the sailors' veins as the ships and their sailors once more came through the firefight unscathed.

For the next ten days *Newport News* steamed continuously. She ran a rigorous schedule back and forth between Task Unit 77.1.2 and Task Unit 70.8.9 in MR1, alternating between daylight and midnight raids up north and gunfire support in the south near the DMZ.

DMZ, "De-Militarized Zone," was actually a misnomer. Since the main thrust of the North Vietnamese Army was to break through the seventeenth parallel and take over South Vietnam, the least accurate adjective to use in describing this region would be "de-militarized." The battle was bloody and constant as the fleet units, riverine patrols, and SEALs of the U.S. Navy were deployed and re-deployed continually, using hit-and-run tactics to stem the overflowing tide of men and munitions from the North. Strategies were employed, altered, and manipulated feverishly to hold ground and give the enemy the impression our forces had increased in size and capability.

It was one tremendous balancing act to rush assets hither and thither in an all-out attempt to respond to rapidly changing situations and maintain control of supply routes and defensive positions. The aircraft carriers kept their maximum effort arrayed against the North as well, and casualties mounted on both the ground inland and in the air above Vietnam. Monsoon rains with heavy cloud covers further complicated the efforts by restricting the number of B-52 strikes.

By the 27th of August the stage had been set for a daring three-pronged naval strike against Haiphong, the Do Son Peninsula, and Cat Ba Island at the mouth of Haiphong Harbor. This carefully calculated effort was named "Operation Lion's Den."

Admiral James L. Holloway III, Commander of the Seventh Fleet, was chosen to conduct the operation from the bridge of the *Newport News*, which would now take on the call-sign "Blackbeard." The Guided Missile Cruiser *USS Providence*, Guided Missile Destroyer *USS Robison,* and the Destroyer *USS Rowan* would complete the strike force. The *Providence* was a smaller cruiser than the *Newport News*. She had a six-inch triple turret plus a five-inch twin mount forward and a Talos missile launcher aft where the rear gun turret had been removed. The Talos launcher could fire two surface-to-surface missiles simultaneously at about ten second intervals, while her forward gun turret could fire six-inch artillery, almost equivalent to the enemy 130mm guns, at a rate similar to *Newport News'* main battery turrets. *USS Robison* had one forward single five-inch mount, another aft, and a missile launcher behind that like those on the *Providence*. Rounding out the flotilla was *USS Rowan*, which was a conventional gun destroyer with one forward and one aft five-inch twin gun mount. *Rowan's* special equipment included anti-radiation radar, which was specially designed to seek out enemy fire control radars and target them and their associated gun positions. It also had two Shrike, anti-radiation missile launchers high up atop the center of her superstructure.

The central element of the Task Unit was *Newport News* with her three triple eight-inch turrets, six twin five-inch mounts, and eight twin three-inch mounts. Together, these made up the most formidable gunship flotilla available in the Seventh Fleet.

Lion's Den was to be the most encompassing naval surface fleet attack on North Vietnam to date. The three target areas included surface-to-air and surface-to-surface missile sites along the Do Son, SAM sites and coastal defense artillery in the Haiphong Harbor complex, and newly added and fortified missile and artillery positions on Cat Ba Island.

In order to strike all three areas in rapid succession, it would be necessary to position the Task Unit in the mouth of the harbor delta, southwest of Cat Ba and east of the Do Son, but far enough north into the harbor delta to reach western Haiphong. This meant the ships would be within firing range of all three positions for most of the operation, and in that position they would be boxed in with artillery firing on them from the west, north, and east. Additionally, they would need to maneuver rapidly through and around shallow shoals, narrow waterways, and previously placed mine fields that had been activated after the first Haiphong Raid on May 10. As the strike plans came together for this operation, the rumor mill aboard *Newport News* went wild.

"My God," Ray said as Dave unrolled the yellow roll. On it was a teletype facsimile in characters and punctuations which depicted the gauntlet proposed. "We can't even zigzag through that channel. They'll have a bead on us all the time. We'll look like ducks on a pond, all in a nice little row. If they pour everything they have into that narrows they have to hit at least one of us."

"That's what I told you," Dave said, "and we're the biggest target. When we start firing we'll be lit up like a homing beacon."

"Shit! Shit! How the hell can we do that? Then we have to turn almost 110, or maybe ninety-five degrees to clear the mine fields."

"That's if they haven't moved them," Dave added.

"What do you mean?"

"There are Intel reports that the Gooks have been moving the mines around with divers and boats so we won't know where they are, so they can use our own mines on us if we come back."

"Oh you've got to be shitting me! Man they're gonna blow us all to hell, they'll cream us."

"They're trying to get SEALs and UDT in there to verify the mine positions, but so far no confirmation on that." His friend continued, "It gets worse Ray. Think about it—if one of the ships gets disabled we'll be all bunched up like a pair of cheap jockey shorts right under their guns. Then if we have to abandon ship, we'll be in waters infested with sharks and sea snakes, and if we manage, after all that, to swim to shore, we'll be in enemy hands."

Dave, always the alarmist, had picked the very worst of the worst-case scenarios possible, but Ray had to agree it wasn't a very far stretch to imagine that happening.

"Fuck me runnin'," Ray said. "I can't believe they're really going to try this. They're putting 2,000 American sailors and Marines at high risk, and the odds are stacked against us to begin with. Think about all those fucking 130 sites, there must be hundreds of them."

"Just shy of three hundred all together," Dave stated, "that's according to aerial recon photos, 130s *and* 155s by the Intel reports."

"No...No, I'm not believing this, this is insanity Dave. They're gonna get us all killed; throw us to the wolves, and let them gobble us up. They can't do that, it's insane."

"Where have you been, brother? Look what we've been doing, we've been jumping them in broad daylight for the past two weeks. This is just another step up."

"Yeah, but that was farther south. This is Haiphong Harbor, *Hai-fucking-phong Harbor*, the largest seaport and most heavily defended place in North Vietnam, next to Hanoi. Hell, what am I saying, this is the sea entrance to Hanoi. Oh my God buddy, we're fucked."

The raid was set to go off at 10:30 p.m., and it was now 8:45 p.m.. The adrenaline buzz ramped up slowly and continuously over the next hour and forty-five minutes. The entire crew became tuned to every sound, every movement the ship made slicing through the waves in the coal-black night. The wind was balmy and heavy with the smell of salt. In ones and twos, men walked topside to have one last look, a smoke, or a poignant conversation with one of their closest buddies. Eyes strained to make out anything in the night, but nothing was out there. There was no moon, no stars, no lights of any type; just the faintest hint of breaking bow waves from the neighboring ships and the hissing sound of the wind, which seemed, for all its subtlety, like the hissing of some huge reptile waiting to swallow them whole.

In the bowels of the ship, in Radio One, in the Combat Information Center, in Commanding Officers Tactical Plot, on the bridge, at the lookout stations, in the fire control directors, and in the ammo handling rooms, men drew long, slow breaths and tried to steady their nerves.

Compulsive bursts of laughter and horse-play broke out spontaneously as anxious young men tried to stem the nervousness and anticipation that was overtaking them like a raging flash-flood cascading down a river canyon. Nothing to be done, no way to stop it; the onslaught was upon them and all they could do was hope and pray.

The words "helpless" and "powerless" had never truly meant anything to Ray until now, but the feeling running though his mind, as the ships once again went to General Quarters and commenced their wicked dance, was utter and complete demoralizing fear.

His thoughts were scattered, his mind raced and skipped through endless scenarios. He thought of Cynthia. *God*, he thought to himself, *I wish I could see her, be back in her arms and wake up realizing this was just a nightmare*. He thought of his Asian lovers, then his parents, then his buddies and friends back home. He prayed earnestly, *Dear God please, please let us get through this alive*. Immediately following that: *I wish Chief Yerks was here for this, I really feel much better when the Chief is here*. The Chief had reached his rotation date and his tour on the *Newport News* had ended. He had been high-lined to one of the service fleet ships two days earlier to be shuttled back to a billet stateside.

Ray glanced at the glowing lights on the electronic equipment surrounding him. He heard a burst of static on one of the tactical voice circuits as someone nervously keyed a mic to ensure his radio was working. He looked at Mike sitting at the monitor station. His eyes were wide open in anticipation, and Commander Stroud was staring into his coffee cup or down at the deck, Ray couldn't tell which. Then the radio circuits barked to life, startling them all.

"Overwork this is Blackbeard, turn starboard four five degrees on my mark. Ready, execute." Silence once again.

Then, two minutes later, "Overwork this is Blackbeard, turn starboard four zero degrees and commence firing on my mark. Ready, execute."

Ba-boom, Ba-boom, Ba-boom, Ba-boom! The rounds started pumping out. In concert came less imposing booms from the five-inchers and still-lighter reports from the neighboring ships. The popcorn popper was ramping up faster and greater than ever before, or so it seemed.

Combat, North Vietnam, June 1972

The eruption continued, gaining in momentum and duration. Then the first of the incoming arrived. Mike's eyes widened as he looked meaningfully at Ray and then back to Commander Stroud. "Holy Shit!" he said. "Damn they're really throwing it at us. You should hear these guys topside."

Ka-thud, Ka-thud. The closest subsurface bursts any of them had yet experienced jarred them. In the center of each burst they could clearly perceive loud, metallic, staccato clunks, which indicated armor-piercing warheads.

The radio came to life: “Blackbeard this is Fighting Devil, we are taking heavy counter battery from our port beam, can you suppress? Over.” There was a pause.

“Blackbeard, Blackbeard, this is Fighting Devil, do you read? Over.”

“Ah…ah…Fighting Devil, this is Blackbeard, I read you, we are taking the same CB, will try to cover you as best we can, out.” The terseness of the last transmission meant, “Don’t bother me, I’m up to my ass in alligators myself.”

“Blackbeard, Blackbeard, this is Vicar. We have a bogie operating surface-to-surface missile radars at 270 degrees relative, request permission to engage, over.”

“Vicar, this is Blackbeard, permission granted, waste the bastards, out.”

“Blackbeard this is Firehorse, over…Blackbeard, Blackbeard this is Firehorse. Firehorse, over.”

“Firehorse this is Blackbeard, contact Blackbeard two on secondary. I say again, switch to the secondary channel and contact Blackbeard two, out.” The chaotic environment required more control, so the Admiral’s staff and Captain Zartman split their resources to accommodate the situation.

Now the secondary tactical secure voice circuit came to life as Blackbeard continued to communicate on the Primary.

“Overwork this is Blackbeard, turn to starboard four five degrees on my mark. Ready, execute.” The ships swung to starboard once more as the barrage of outgoing and incoming artillery continued. The secondary channel came alive again.

“Blackbeard two this is Firehorse, I have surface contacts bearing three five zero degrees relative at four five knots, can you get a visual confirmation on them? Over.”

“Ah, this is Blackbeard two, I’ll have my people scan for confirmation. Out.” Seconds later the sound powered phone circuit came alive. “All hands this is the captain, we have reports of high-speed, surface contacts bearing three five zero relative, I want all eyes scanning that bearing.”

The incoming intensified. It seemed like the rate of incoming was greater than the outgoing salvos, and the metallic clunks grew more frequent.

“Blackbeard two this is Firehorse. I’m firing Shrikes at target bearing two zero five degrees relative.”

“This is Blackbeard two, Roger.”

Ray was becoming so hyped that his ears were ringing. The information coming in was fast and furious, and his mind perceived only sketches of what was happening as he tried to maintain composure and listen for signs of circuit deterioration. A succession of rapid static bursts came over the primary tactical circuit. He looked at the speaker and waited. Again the speaker burst a long period of static as the phone in Radio One started ringing.

"Radio One, may I help you?" Ray answered. The voice on the other end sounded shaken.

"This is the bridge. We've just lost our primary tac-com, we need it back now."

"Use the Prick-25 portable," Ray responded, "I'll get it back ASAP." The phone clicked, and Ray hung up his end and ran to the switching panel. He found the patches and turned the knobs to switch to the backup equipment, then he heard the Primary come to life again.

"Overwork this is Blackbeard. Turn to starboard one five degrees and commence contingency alpha on my command. Ready, execute."

Ray had no idea what contingency alpha was, nor did he need to know. He ran back to the intercom, depressed the PTT switch, and announced, "Bridge this is Radio One, you have your primary back." His ears picked up the familiar dit-dit of static as someone, obviously harried and pressed for time, just keyed the intercom switch in response.

Contingency alpha was one of three proposed escape plans. They had been in a raging firefight for twelve minutes running now and the pressure from the shore batteries was still increasing. When contingency alpha was executed, the ships fanned out on five-degree intervals and steamed for thirty seconds to get enough space between them to commence independent zigzag courses, each still firing and returning fire from the enemy defenses.

"Damn!" came an excited voice on the SPP circuit, amid background sounds of expletives and surprise, "something just blew there, it looks like an ammo dump or something."

"Shit!"

"Look at that! The whole place is going up."

"Blackbeard, Blackbeard, Blackbeard, this is Fighting Devil, we have a fix on those surface contacts, they are closing on you at figures three thousand yards, relative bearing two nine zero off your port bow, over."

"Roger, Fighting Devil, this is Blackbeard, we see them now, can you identify them? Over." The incoming rounds began to subside, in frequency and proximity; it appeared the flotilla was leaving them behind.

"PT boats," Mike yelped, "PT boats coming at us full bore. The watches can see their wakes, there are two or three of them." Mike pulled both earphones over his ears now to listen more intently. The Russian-made Patrol Torpedo boats were fast, maneuverable, and deadly if they got within range to launch torpedoes. Each boat carried four of the screaming death machines. These submarine bombs, each with a 2000-pound warhead, were capable of sinking a ship with just one good hit. Now there were twelve of them being readied for launch by their boat crews racing to meet the Task Unit.

The ships began to zigzag, listing sharply from one side to the other. The rate of fire of *Thunder*'s guns had just begun to subside when, suddenly, there was resurgence. Turrets one and two opened up, mount fifty-one and fifty-two began pumping rounds again, now the three-inch twins were popping off.

"They're coming on fast," Mike reported, "2,000 yards and closing, they think they're attacking. Holy Shit, man, they're catching up fast."

"Blackbeard, Blackbeard, this is Firehorse, Firehorse," the secondary tactical circuit came to life once more.

"Firehorse this is Blackbeard, go ahead, over."

"This is Firehorse, have bogies inbound at fifteen miles bearing two two zero degrees relative. Suspect they are enemy aircraft over."

"Roger Firehorse, stand by your Redeye launchers."

"Overwork this is Blackbeard, be advised we have incoming enemy aircraft bearing two two zero degrees relative at one five miles, activate anti-aircraft systems now and prepare to launch on any non-squawkers."

Ray could not keep his composure any longer. He stood up from the watch desk and yelled at the speakers, "What the fuck, we're being attacked by artillery, PT boats, and aircraft all at the same time?"

The Redeye, anti-aircraft missile launchers were positioned on the shoulders of several Marines and sailors on each ship. The search button was flipped, and the gyros began to whine in the missile guidance systems. These small, but effective, shoulder-launched weapons would seek out the hot exhaust gases coming form any aircraft within four miles of their position and track to it, exploding on contact, it was hoped.

The circuits remained abuzz with chatter and continued to crescendo with each passing moment. Ray started to feel as if he were floating away from the scene and leaving it all behind. Everything seemed to fall to the background; time seemed to move slower and slower. The sounds grew faint as the buzz in his ears increased, and the pounding of blood to his temples grew. All movement resembled slow-motion cinematography; Mike was speaking, but no sound came from his lips. Commander Stroud walked down the middle of the space toward the switchboard and turned back with an inquisitive look on his face. Ray gazed at the coffee sloshing in his cup on the desk in front of him. Coffee splashed over its rim as the cup slid sideways.

Suddenly everything accelerated into hyper-speed as the piercing sound of high-pitched electronic squealing jarred his consciousness.

"The KY-14 dropped sync!" Mike shouted excitedly. "Get the KY-14, Ray!" Ray sprinted past the Commander and flipped a switch on the patch panel and returned to the watch desk gazing at the status board. There had been no outage; the people needing to use the circuits had their backup portables within easy reach and communications continued uninterrupted, albeit chaotic. Ray took the grease pencil and rag, and calmly and mechanically erased the column where the defective crypto gear was listed and put an asterisk on the backup equipment column. Then he reached for his coffee and took a sip.

He didn't know what had happened, but suddenly he felt calm and peaceful. He was not shaken; he didn't feel any fear. He didn't say a word, he just sipped his coffee and gazed around the room again. Commander Stroud was walking back to his previous position and taking a sip from his coffee cup. Mike just stared at Ray with glassy eyes. Ray stepped into the control space and slowly and deliberately began to run through the reset procedure on the KY-14 that had fallen out of synchronization. It went through its normal routine and paused, as always, before the green light blinked on indicating it was reset and ready to use again.

Some sort of transformation had come over him. The noise and chatter was as chaotic as ever, but he no longer felt its urgency. He was numb, emotionless, and calm. The phone rang at the watch desk and he walked to it and answered, "Radio One, may I help you, Sir?" An excited voice said, "I think we lost the primary tac-com circuit again, we're using the backup."

"We had an equipment failure down here," Ray said calmly, "you're back online with the primary again." There was a pause. Ray could hear the chaos on the bridge. There were expletives and excited shouts and booms from the forward turrets. The person on the other end replied, "OK, ah, thanks," and hung up.

It was nothing he had consciously done. In fact, Ray had no idea what had happened to him. Maybe his mind had overloaded. Whatever it was, he liked it. It was as if he had just received a huge dose of a strong sedative. He felt calm and euphoric. He sat down and finished his coffee and contemplated his comfort.

It's OK, he thought to himself. *Whatever happens now, it's OK, I'm gonna be all right.*

Ten minutes later they were standing around and talking. The guns had stopped booming, the ships had stopped listing, they were following a swift course away from the action, and everyone began to settle down.

The 1MC crackled to life and Captain Zartman spoke, "Ah…this is the captain, I'd like to start out by saying, you guys are the absolute best! Ah…when I promised a little excitement I didn't realize we were going to have this much. We fired 1,000 rounds…we came in first, ah…we were dropped down to a total of seven main battery targets and the three CD (coastal defense) sites. As we came out, what now appears to have been three PT boats started closing from the east off our port bow. We believe that our initial fire, we're certain that it at least damaged and stopped the first one; whether it sank, we do not know. The other two continued to close, actually got within range of where they could have pickled off a torpedo. Would have been their maximum range. We ah…slowed them down. We got one and we believe that *Rowan*, who was just ahead of us, stopped the second one. We got tactical air in, and ah…we don't know what they did, but we presume we can scratch three PT boats for the night.

"I want to say, I really mean it, that everybody did a tremendous job—from the people making the steam down there in those fire-rooms, the lookouts who gave us the first indication of PT boats, the radar men who were right on top of it at the same time, the signal men, people plotting fixes up here, and positions that were dangerously close to shoal water. I could go on and on and on, but, ah…and the gunners were really tremendous. They were in there, as guns went down they were getting them up right away. Ah…we had a lot of rounds to get off in a short time. T-three was absolutely fabulous back there by coming in to give a hand on more targets than they had scheduled, and of course, they were our get away gun when we were being chased down the pike here by the three PT boats.

"It, ah…it couldn't have been improved upon, I think, ah…and I hope that this is the most exciting night we have while we're out here. Thank you again, every one of you."

As the adrenaline rush slowed down for the remainder of the crew, Ray stayed right in his euphoric shell. Stories circulated around the ship, and by daybreak all had learned the remaining details of the raid.

The enemy aircraft, presumably MIG 17s or 21s, had come within ten or so miles and turned back, probably having realized that they would be tangling with well-armed and prepared ships. There were also air patrols flying guard over the ships to dissuade them further. The preliminary reports were that all targets had been hit and severely damaged or taken out completely—another clean sweep for the night raiders of TU 77.1.2.

In the morning, after breakfast, Ray walked the main deck. The morning sunlight was breaking through the scattered clouds as he smoked a couple of cigarettes before returning to his rack. He felt aloof, distant, dazed, and serene, and he couldn't quite understand why, but he slept very well and woke well rested at 5:00 p.m.

Chapter 19

The Berkeley Effect

Ray felt much different. He ate a leisurely meal, sitting by himself in one corner of the mess decks. He then took a long, slow walk forward on the starboard side of the main deck. It was balmy still; multiple layers of scattered clouds with high altitude overcast sailed above them. *Thunder* was moving at medium speed and he could hear a gentle sloshing of the waves striking her hull above the waterline. The rolling waves were probably six to eight feet in height from crest to troths. The old girl rocked lazily as her bow plunged in deeper with the rising swells.

He didn't know what it was that was different. He just sensed that something had changed. Last night, when all the pressure and stress came down on him at once, when he felt there was no way out and the end was near, something snapped and his whole outlook had been re-adjusted. But he couldn't quite tell what the difference was. He knew he didn't feel anxious, he didn't feel afraid; he really didn't know what he felt.

That's it, Ray thought, *I don't feel. I don't really feel anything.* It was just a fleeting thought, nothing like an epiphany.

Actually, a fair number of the crew was feeling the same way. Some of the topside people and sailors on the bridge and weapons stations had also reached their limit. They had stared death in the face enough times already that this one last big push over the edge had numbed them. They had accepted that sooner or later it would be their time. They had gone beyond the fear and emotion to a place where they had no doubt they were going to die at some point, it was just a question of when.

For twenty-year-olds, this is a hard barrier to break through. Until now they had believed themselves invincible, strong, and immortal. They had believed that they could accomplish anything. Their leaders constantly reinforced this belief. But as young adults, they were also logical. It was plain to see, and had been demonstrated many times, that there were real and intense circumstances surrounding their activities. Many of them realized that the placement or misplacement of enemy salvos, along with surface craft and aircraft threats, was unpredictable. Pushing the envelope became more and more precarious as time passed.

They had just squeaked by once more. How many times would they just *happen* to be in a place where the salvos didn't land? How long they were going to continue and how often the process would be repeated were the variables in the equation. Many of the men began to feel they were living on borrowed time. Many of them began to write morbid, poignant letters to their closest loved ones, clearing up any unspoken or unresolved issues. Some of them became less reactive, less responsive, and less aware. Zombie-like behaviors started to become prevalent. Dark humor began to run in circles around the ship. "What's the difference between a *Thunder* sailor and a hamburger?" "About ten yards" was the answer, alluding to the placement of a salvo of 155mm bombs.

"Fuck it" became the most common term when any little thing didn't go right in their personal lives. The implication: it doesn't matter anyway, we'll be dead before much longer.

Sometimes the psychological stresses evoked a different response. Mike was standing at his locker one day trying to open it with the same combination lock he had used daily for the last one and a half years. No one noticed he was there until he exploded and started screaming and yelling profanities, pounding the aluminum locker door with his fists. By the time his tirade had subsided, the locker looked like it had been hit by a truck. All those watching fell silent as Mike stomped out of the compartment and bolted topside.

Strikes of lesser magnitude continued along with rigorous gunfire support missions in the south. 1,000-round days became more common. But somehow they made it through, and by September 11 they were once again headed back to Subic, and then word spread that they had been diverted to Hong Kong for liberty.

On the day they left the gun line, Ray was walking topside with Bird, having a smoke. The sky was blue and the guns were popping and booming in the lazily moving destroyer and cruiser fleet offshore in MR1. Huge palls of smoke rose from various places on the beach. Looking toward Vietnam, they could see ships close in along the swaying palm trees and white beaches, shelling positions inland amid the dense green jungle. B-52 bombings were continuing often. The reverberations that had become familiar to the sailors shook the ships.

After one of these bombings, when the ship was close to the shore, Bird and Ray rushed to the starboard side of the ship to see actual flashes of light and fire as the position was attacked by a second wave of bombers. They observed this for a few minutes and Bird stepped into the hatch that led to Radio One to return to his watch.

Ray strolled forward and noticed Bobby, one of their gang, sitting on a mooring cleat just forward of turret two. He was gazing dream-like at the war as if stunned and aloof. Ray hailed him from several yards away as he approached his friend.

"Yo, Bobby, what's up?" There was no response. Stepping to within a few feet of him Ray repeated. "Bobby, hey, what's up dude?"

As his friend turned, Ray could see tears flowing down his cheeks. Small wet spots on his t-shirt showed where fallen tears had landed. He had been crying for some time.

"What's wrong Bobby? Are you OK? What's the matter buddy?" Ray saw a letter where Bobby's left hand rested on his left thigh.

"We're fucked brother," Bobby blurted out, "we're fucking totally fucked, and we're assholes for being here and doing what we're doing. I can't believe I got sucked into this clusterfuck." He was sobbing uncontrollably now.

"Bobby, hey buddy, don't let it get to you. We're doing what we have to do. We may be totally fucked, but we're doing this so the people back home don't ever have to go through the kind of shit these poor South Vietnamese people are going through. We have to do this, someone has to stop it."

"Bullshit, Ray! That's all bullshit, we're causing this thing to happen. This war is all about power. We're perpetrating this thing just to get what we want out of Southeast Asia, there are resources here we're trying to tap. People say there are great oil resources off shore here. I don't know what it is, but it's all our fault, we're just a part of a great big, military machine. We're the aggressors, not the Vietnamese."

"Bobby, what are you talking about? You know that's not true."

"Do I? Read this." He handed Ray the letter.

Dear Bobby,

I don't even know how to begin honey. I have to write this, and I want to say things as honestly as I can and I pray you will not be hurt by it, but at the same time I know it is impossible that you won't. So what can I do? I have thought long and hard and talked to many people about how I feel, and everyone tells me I have to do what is right for both of us. I kept hoping there was some other way.

Wow, Ray thought, *she gets right to the point, no mistaking where this is going.*

So here goes, I'm sure you already know what's coming, I'm so sorry baby, I can't change it. I am breaking our engagement. Things have changed; I've changed and you have changed, and we can never be the same people we were before. Remember I begged you to stay in college, fight the draft, and not join the Navy? We could have gone to Canada until this was all over with. Anyway, I can't live this way any longer. Here at Berkeley things are all different than back in Michigan. The people here really know what's going on. The California people know better than anybody else what a farce this war is.

If you had only listened and come with me I know you would have made different choices. But it's too late for that. You have been sucked into something you didn't know about. I don't blame you Bobby, I know you thought you were doing the right thing, but this whole thing is a government conspiracy to take control of Vietnam and the whole of Southeast Asia. It is wrong, I know it is, I've learned and become enlightened. I can see through the camouflage the government is throwing up to conceal it.

My Poli. Sci. prof. is leading a movement that is going to expose all of the corruption and control the government is perpetrating. She is a major figure here at Berkeley and is going to help Jane Fonda expose the bastards. Do you listen to Jane? They say she's broadcasting over there where you guys are right now. Listen to her Bobby, she really knows what she's saying. If you would just think about it, I know you'd see she's right.

You could listen Bobby and think about it. I know if you just thought about it you'd come to your senses. I don't mean to say you're brainwashed or anything, but this is all a very cleverly conceived plan, and the military is feeding you guys a whole pile of junk about it.

You could leave and come back here if you wanted. We could go to Canada, lots of other people have, and I know some who are really glad they made the choice to be there.

Darling, I do still love you, or who you were, but I can't stay with someone who is involved in this terrible deception, even unwittingly. I have too many feelings about its ethics. We all have faith, yeah, that's right, me I know the Lord now, and he is smiling on me, and you too if you make the right choice. I wish you would just go on leave or take off or something and come back to me, but after your last few letters I realized you have changed. You actually sounded proud of doing what you're doing. I can't conceive of that. Do you know there are thousands of innocent people being killed by what you're doing? Listen to what Jane is saying Bobby, just listen to her, the people of North Vietnam are peaceful, agricultural people; they don't hurt anyone, they just want to be left alone and you guys are killing them. I'm sorry Bobby, I can't say any more, it makes me sick to think about it. I know you won't change your mind, you are too stubborn and you think you're right. Don't you see, that's why I have to do this?

I don't want you to write back. I don't want to hurt you, but it can only hurt both of us more if we keep trying to go on like this. Maybe someday we will meet again and things will be different.

Goodbye Bobby. I love you and I'm sorry, but goodbye. I have to tell you I have a new boyfriend, and he and I will work our hardest to make sure you guys get back home.

Trust in the Lord Bobby,
Lisa

Christ! Ray thought, *why don't you kick him in the teeth a few more times? I don't think he's stopped breathing yet.* Ray held the letter for a few more minutes.

"She's right, isn't she Ray?" he said. "This is just one big, total clusterfuck, and we're just little pawns doing the dastardly duty, just like Uncle Sam and Nixon want us to. Like little ants scurrying here and there, going about the grunt work. And when someone comes along and steps on us and kills us all off, we'll just be another load of ground up dirt and a bunch of other little ants will come in and take over the job. Meanwhile, we just keep killing those people. Do you realize there are people dying out there? Those are people we're shooting at Ray. How can we do this?"

"I don't know Bobby, I don't know," were the most eloquent words Ray could muster. "Fuck Jane Fonda! Fuck the world, Bobby, just fuck it! We're going to Hong Kong to get good and fucked up and laid. That's all I know." As crass as it seemed, it was probably the only thing that helped Bobby focus on anything but his troubles, even if just for a while.

It took three days to get to Hong Kong. Ray and Bobby talked frequently. Bobby ranged from hyperactive to depressive and from listless to suicidal. His eyes were red from crying and lack of sleep.

"Fuck it Bobby, just stick with me," Ray said, "we're going to get so blistered we won't see straight, and we're going to shack up with a couple of Chinese girls that'll make us feel like we died and went to heaven."

A couple of times Bobby chuckled. He was a cherry and had never been with any of the girls from Subic. He had held on to his loyalty to Lisa with every ounce of restraint he could muster. Other times he just passed the idea off as useless.

"I don't want to have anything to do with any woman," he said. "I don't think I will love anyone again, and I think the whole idea of love is a crock of shit. Jesus! We spent four years together Ray—now she's throwing me out like an old pair of socks. She's enlightened," he added with stinging sarcasm, "she's found the Lord, yeah right, and he probably has an eight-inch dick and hair down to his ass."

"She's a college sophomore, Bobby, it's her first time away from home. She's young and impressionable, trying to find some reason in all of this shit. Hell, she's right in the middle of hippie heaven and sucking up every bit of that culture. You can't blame her Bobby, she thinks, like many do, that they have found the answer. It's simple enough—they think war sucks. They think 'war kills people, we have evolved beyond that, so there is no excuse for ever having wars again.' They live in California, back in the world, remember? Most of them have never even been out of the country. Hell Bobby, Cynthia keeps writing me about the demonstrations that are happening on campus where she is in Stroudsburg, Pennsylvania. She doesn't agree with them, but who knows, that could change, she's only eighteen. We can't expect them to see things the way we do or really know what is going on here when there is so much confusion and controversy about it. Hell, Bobby, we don't even get a clear picture of any of this, how can we expect them to?

'We're living in the Age of Aquarius, the age of enlightenment, we have found the answers. Our generation of Americans has suddenly become the ones who finally understand, or so some people think. Aside from a large penis and long hair, I wouldn't doubt if Jesus has lots of enlightening remedies as well," Ray said, implying the drug culture of the west coast. Ray felt like an older brother trying to comfort a sibling who had experienced his first heartbreak.

"Yeah, I guess you're right. The bitch of it is, Ray, I'm stuck here and can't do a fucking thing about it. All I can do is live with it, along with everything else I'm expected to live with. That's the thing that really sucks about being here. Maybe she's right, I should have gone to Canada and told Uncle Sam to eat shit. 'Be a man!' my father said, 'I did my time in World War II, that's what a real man does. When our country calls on us we go to bat for it.' Fuck you, Dad!"

Bobby's voice fell silent as he continued staring at the green floor tiles on the deck of the compartment. Ray left his friend to contemplate and took a walk topside for a smoke.

Maybe Bobby is right, maybe Lisa is right, he thought to himself. *Maybe Hanoi Jane is right. Maybe we're all fucked up and there is no real reason for this piece of shit war except war. Oil reserves? Control of Southeast Asia? Who knows. If so, it will come to light at some point, and we'll go down in history as the biggest bunch of maniacal bastards since Hitler. Won't that be a fuck story—how I spent my time in the Navy of the Fourth Reich!*

They arrived in Hong Kong on a sunny day with puffy clouds. Most of the men of *Thunder* had accumulated considerable wealth in terms of enlisted men in the service. With no place to spend their tax-free combat pay, which was thirty or so percent higher than normal, lots of time at sea meant ample opportunity for the pay to accrue. Everyone had five days of excess on the mind, whether in the dark and dingy realm of debauchery, or with less immoral pursuits. For the Pagan among them, this issue was less clearly defined. Sailors were sailors. To many that was the only credo worth holding onto. For many of them, the term "fuck it" was all that applied.

Chapter 20

Chaos and Calm

Hong Kong came and went and the five days of R&R were rejuvenating. Once again the crew of the mighty *Thunder* had a chance to satisfy their appetites with world-class, international cuisine and spirits of all varieties. The same held true for their sexual appetites, though the Hong Kong women were not quite as accommodating or as inexpensive as in Subic Bay. No matter. Few of the crew objected to the escalated prices.

Leaving Hong Kong, they went back to Subic for another four days of maintenance. Ray reached the age of twenty-one as the 19th found him and his buddies celebrating at the NCO club on base. *Thunder* finally returned to the war zone on September 23.

Leaving their "home away from home" they returned to Vietnam. Not much had changed. MR1 was still a mass of smoke and fire. Slowly moving gun ships still rattled off sporadic salvos and then repositioned to reach specific targets. It was business as usual. Ray and Mike had rotated to the day watch while Bird and Don took the night watches.

Rejoining TU 77.1.1 in the late night and early morning hours of September 24–25, *Thunder* made raids on the North Vietnamese areas of Than Hoa and Vinh. She was a coastal raider once again and bounced back and forth between quick-paced strikes and her dreary support role.

The evening of September 30 found them at MR1 with orders to conduct a midnight attack on North Vietnamese forces dug in twelve kilometers north of the battlefront. They expected to take counter battery from enemy field artillery arrayed along the coastal side of the highlands, defending the invasion force massing for another push south.

Ray was complacent and numb again. He felt the whole thing was anti-climactic. It wasn't a coordinated, high-speed raid like the ones in the far north. He watched the newsreel footage supplied on the compartment television over the ships internal TV network and critiqued, along with others, the misleading reports journalists had been manipulated to produce.

Jesus, he thought to himself, *the way those guys talk we have this thing all sewn up, and we'll be going home next week. That's not what it looks like from the main deck.* Sarcasm had become his main defense.

More of the "fuck-its" had crept into the psyches of the men and officers. Ray even heard snide remarks or brief expletive comments on the radio circuits as the fleet conducted its deadly missions. They felt like they were living in a limbo-like underworld where the sun was obscured by smoke, and the air was pungent with the smell of death. Anger and frustration overcame many of them. Some began to listen to the broadcasts of anti-war activists like Hanoi Jane (Fonda) and focus on news items and magazine articles about the increasing demonstrations back home.

Morale is at a low point, Ray thought to himself as he read the last of Homer's *Odyssey* and snapped the light off in his private sanctuary. He contemplated Odysseus's feelings. *I understand wanting to move so far inland that no one would know the meaning of the word "oar,"* he thought. *I think I'd like to move to the isolated regions of far north Canada, myself.* He rolled over, thought of Cynthia for a moment, and drifted off to sleep. He dozed in and out of deep slumbers, almost, but not quite aware of the staccato bursts of the ship's outgoing salvos. Then once more it would be quiet, dreamy, and comfortable.

Wah-Booooom! The sound penetrated his deep sleep, and he had a sense of the immense pressure wave that accompanied the explosion. The sound was not quite consciously in his grasp, it was just barely out of reach, a vague disturbance as he slept.

Suddenly, the compartment fire-watch was shaking him and shouting: "Get up! Get up! Everybody get up and get a gas mask. We've been hit! We're on fire! Get your Mark 5s on." Another early responder shoved a Mark 5 filter mask into Ray's bunk. "Put this on quick, and get to your GQ station."

The claxons started blatting, and the warning bells were gonging loudly. The 1MC came to life with a loud burst: "General Quarters! General Quarters! All hands man your battle stations, set Condition Zebra throughout the ship, General Quarters! Dog all watertight doors and hatches...." The announcement continued to repeat as men scrambled out of their bunks, adjusted their gas masks, and pulled on their clothes.

The compartment filled with a thick caustic-smelling smoke. Ray saw the red battle lamps positioned around the bulkheads at about knee level. The CR division compartment was closed and dogged down tight, and the watches were guiding the waking men through the cross-ship passageway to the starboard side and yelling, "Forward and up on the starboard side. Aft and down on the Port side. Get to your GQ stations ASAP. Walk, don't run. Move in an orderly fashion. This is not a drill, I say again, this is not a drill. Go to your GQ stations immediately. You'll get further instructions at your GQ stations. Do not go topside. Stay clear of the main deck forward of the sickbay area."

Ray heard excited voices as he made his way up the starboard berthing compartment ladder and through the circular hatch behind a row of radio and signal department crewmembers, all wearing gas masks. Once into the passageway he saw hose crews. The firemen moved frantically forward, dragging their heavy hoses through opened cross-ship doors to the port side. Smoke billowed from opening doors and hatches as he moved forward.

Men were barking orders and yelling responses to questions from their superiors. The rush of water through fire hoses as the hydrants were opened indicated great pressure and speed. Water spouted from fittings along the hoses lying on the deck. Clanging and dogging of doors could be heard from all directions. Men yelled excitedly, some with fear in their voices, others cool and calm as if they had expected this and it was no shock at all to them.

Ray worked mechanically toward the forward part of the ship. As he did, the smoke became thicker. Damage control crews moved quickly past him. Firefighters shoved past him. "Out of the way sailor," one yelled through his gas mask just inches from Ray's head. "Step aside, step aside, coming through with a hose."

"Gang way, step aside," was another's ongoing monologue. Ray ducked and dodged as he continued forward, straining to see as the illuminated clouds of smoke swirled in reddish puffs like flames lapping and stabbing at him.

I'm heading right into this, he thought. The smoke became thicker and the shouts grew louder as he went forward.

"Open those main deck hatches," yelled a firefighter, "we've got to get this smoke out of here."

Holy Shit, Ray thought, *I'm going right into this, maybe I'd better go topside and back.* Then he remembered the instructions of the compartment watch, "*Go to your GQ station." But what if that's where the fire is? Shit! The fire must be near the main battery turrets, which are all ammo handling rooms and weapons equipment*, he thought.

"Where are you headed sailor?" a voice boomed. "This is all damage control activity here, you can't go further forward on this deck."

"Radio One," Ray stammered, "it's my GQ station."

"I don't know if you can get down there." Ray peered at the Chief Petty Officer through the thick smoke. The Chief must have been wearing a sound powered phone set, he was talking to someone, then he turned to Ray straining to speak through the OBA (oxygen breathing apparatus).

"You can go down through this hatch and through the officer's ward room, then forward and down through the next hatch to Radio One. Stay out of the way of the hose crews."

Ray opened the steel hatch with the quick-acting rotary wheel, and lowered himself down to the ladder below. Smoke streamed in around him as he closed the hatch and stepped down to the deck. There was little to see here, but the smoke was much less dense and he moved forward quickly, opened the next watertight door where a blast of hot smoke burst toward him, and continued forward to another hatch in the deck. Ray reached down, spinning the steel wheel with his left hand. The hatch came open to a bright fluorescent light. Wisps of smoke curled around him and down into the void below. He lowered himself and then realized he was hanging in the hatch without any footing. As he got his bearings, he recognized that his feet were only about twenty-four inches above a familiar surface, the top of one of the vox station desks in the after corner of Radio One. He dropped though the hatch, pulling it down and spinning its wheel to clamp it shut.

Commander Stroud and Don stared at him.

"How did you get up here?" the Commander asked, "I thought the passageways were sealed off."

"They had enough doors open to get firefighting teams through, so I just squeezed in around them. What's happening, where did we get hit?"

"We don't know too many details yet," Don said. "Turret two exploded and is on fire, they're flooding the surrounding ammo handling rooms. I don't think the fire's out, you can hear the steel snapping and banging. I think it's expanding from the heat."

As the words came from his mouth there was a loud bang like a huge object hitting the bulkhead just on the other side of the wall from where they stood. Bird came striding in through the main entrance. "The watertight door into the forward trunk is getting hot, Sir. I think there's water on the other side of it. What should we do, Sir?"

"Just keep calm son, we're stuck here for now. It won't do anyone any good to lose our heads," Stroud eyed the bulkheads and ceiling.

The four of them stood silently for a moment. Then Bird looked at Ray. "You should have gone back to the fantail Ray. If the ammo goes off, we're all dead, we're fucked."

Ray looked at Bird, then across to Don, and then to his left at Commander Stroud. Again the feeling came over him. The bangs and clangs, rushing water, hissing steam, and faint smell of charred materials began to fade away. Once again, all animation blended into slow and methodical movement as if he were watching a scene in a silent movie. The men looked in different directions: Don turned toward the coffeepot, Bird to the outboard wall of Radio One where the R-390 receivers blinked and glowed, their backlit tuning dials suspended as if in a dream. Ray turned back toward the corner cubby he had just entered through. In one corner, several international orange life vests were stacked neatly with nylon mesh bands holding them to the end of one of the operator's desks. Ray stepped toward them and unbuckled the straps. He laid two of the large, puffy vests on the floor and reached back for two more. He arranged them in an elongated pile on the deck and stooped down to pat them as if testing their fluff. Then he lowered himself down onto them and lay down, pulling a fifth one from the pile and placing it under his head. He lay back and arranged the pile a little further for comfort.

Bird looked at him and said, "Ray, what are you doing?"

"I'm beat, Bird. I just have to get some sleep."

Bird and Don looked down at Ray, and then up again at each other in astonishment, their mouths agape. Commander Stroud bent over his mug of coffee and took another sip as he looked at Ray and nodded his approval without showing any surprise. That was the last thing Ray remembered as he drifted off to sleep amid the sounds and reverberations of the chaotic activity around him. He closed his eyes and thought to himself, *Fuck it.*

He slept there for four and a half hours.

Chapter 21

The Dead and the Demoralized

It was the morning of October 1, 1972. Ray awakened to the sound of hissing air as the hatch above his head was opened, the same hatch he had come through five hours earlier. A fresh smell of sea air found its way into the room as he stirred on the life vests. His neck hurt from sleeping on the makeshift bed. A sailor in utility uniform peered down at him through the opened hatch, then turned and disappeared, leaving the hatch open. Then he heard the sound of the watertight door opening at the main entrance to Radio One. The smell of acrid smoke still lingered in the air. Two firefighters poked their heads in to greet the eight men incarcerated in Radio One and classified control. The 1MC sputtered and came to life.

"This is the captain speaking." His tone was soft and fatigued. "We have secured from General Quarters and are proceeding at once to Subic. I can't give you exact numbers or details yet, but it looks like we have in the neighborhood of twenty casualties, that is, twenty dead and another forty or so injured or disabled by smoke inhalation. I respectfully request that anyone other than the damage control personnel and corpsmen (medical staff) stay clear of the area forward of mounts fifty-two and fifty-three. There are activities ongoing to recover the bodies of our lost souls. Additionally, we'll need to stay clear of the flight deck so medivac helos can carry out the operations involving evacuating the wounded. I'll keep you all updated as things develop. For now it's pretty certain the ship is intact, and we should be able to make it back to Subic without any difficulty. Again, I ask you to please respect the rights of the dead by staying clear of the recovery activities if you do not have a job to do near the area. Thank you."

When Ray had gone to sleep he had believed that his death was imminent, that it was only minutes or hours before the magazines blew and the ship went up in one last eruption of fire, smoke, and steel. He had accepted that and decided to go without a fight. Figuring the only survivors would be the people on the opposite end of the ship, he didn't envy any of them the demise they might come to later, and so he decided to stay put and accept what came. He could not conceive of Radio One, immediately adjacent to the raging fire, being a place where anyone would survive. Instead, his mind shut down and let fatigue and his newfound euphoria take him into a sanctuary of blissful sleep.

Now he had opened his eyes to a new day, one he had not expected to see. He was relieved, surprised, and questioned if it was real. The feeling reminded him of the uncertainty he had once felt after having a nightmare in which the ship had been engulfed in a fiery, hot, nuclear explosion. He had lain in is bed in a cold sweat. His heart raced and he couldn't decide if he should open his eyes to see if it was real.

Bird walked quietly back in his direction. Their eyes met and Bird quickly looked away, uncertain how to react, not knowing what Ray's state of mind was. Bird paused for a moment and turned back toward Ray. "We made it through my friend, I thought we had bought the farm. Were you really sleeping?"

"No lie, what happened?"

"I don't believe you could have slept through that. How could you do that? Do you realize what has happened?"

"I couldn't think about it Bird, I just had to turn my thoughts off. I figured we were done. How the hell did we survive?"

"As far as they can tell, a shell exploded inside turret two. I guess everyone in the turret and handling rooms was killed instantly either by the initial explosion and fire, or seconds later when the turret was flooded. They say the ammo caught fire, and the fire got back down into the magazine, but didn't ignite anything else with the exception of a few powder casings. None of the warheads went off except the initial one in the barrel of the gun."

Ray listened as Bird continued.

"I guess the captain was on the bridge, recognized the problem instantly, and ordered the turret flooded, but someone else said the flooding was automatic. Whichever, everybody from the turret down was either burned to a crisp or drowned."

"But there aren't twenty guys in the turret are there?"

"No, only eight of them were in the turret and handling rooms. The others suffocated in berthing compartments. From what I can gather, the smoke immediately filled the first couple of frames aft of the turret, and no one was able to respond quickly enough. They died in their sleep."

Ray thought for a moment how fortunate he was that CR Division was three compartments back from the turret. As the ship had filled with smoke, from the number two turret aft, and the poisonous, caustic fumes and dense smoke poured through its single opened hatch, the suffocating mixture grew less dense and took longer to fill each succeeding space.

"What about our guys?" Ray meant the members of CR Division.

"Swanny, Mac, and Larson were evacuated on the first chopper, don't have any reports back, but we think they're going to be OK."

"How did this happen, Bird?"

"Who knows? Some people are saying sabotage, think maybe the gooks got a funky shell into our arsenal in Subic, or snuck something onboard in Hong Kong. Others are saying something was defective. One of the first reports from the turret said the breach of the center gun was open, and the shell fired back into the turret, but nobody knows anything for sure."

"God," Ray said, "it's a miracle the whole damn ship didn't go up. The old man probably saved us all if his quick action is what stopped the fire. He'll probably get the medal of honor or something."

"Yeah, I guess he's a pretty spry old bird. We could all have been breakfast for the sharks by now if not for him."

The day dragged on. Meals were delayed by other priorities, and it wasn't until 10:00 a.m. that the first of the crew was able to have something to eat. The fire crews and medical department took priority and the mess deck hands began distributing boxed lunches for men who were unable to leave their watch stations or who were engaged in recovery activities, though few of the latter had any appetite for food.

The aftermath was horrible. The four men inside the turret had been burned, literally to a crisp. All the moisture in their bodies had been boiled dry, and their remains were parched to a cinder, their skin appearing light gray or lavender. Their hair had burned off, and a light coating of ash covered their upper bodies where their tee shirts had been. Remnants of ashen cloth strips clung to their lifeless bodies from the waist down. Strips of heavier material from their web belts and shoes were baked dry and solidified into hard masses of smoldering material. So charred were their remains that identification was nearly impossible. The recovery crews who removed them from the turret remarked to others that the bodies had only weighed a fraction of their normal weight. One person could lift any of the corpses with just one hand, and the charred remains had been rendered rigid as though made from papier-mâché. The stench was incredible.

It was estimated that inside the turret the temperature had reached several thousand degrees. The initial explosion was not all that had fueled the fire. Powder casings in the turret, which were ready to cycle into the breaches of the guns, caught fire in the extreme heat. Some of these in turn cascaded down the ammo hoists toward the magazine handling rooms below. Had the turret not been flooded with sea water from the bottom up, there would have been no stopping the chain reaction that would have ripped through the adjacent ammo bunkers and blown the entire front half of the ship skyward.

The bodies of the men down lower in the turret barbet, where the ammo was being loaded onto hoists used for the auto-loading process, showed signs of both sudden, intense burning heat and complete submergence in seawater. It looked as though one or two of them had been unharmed by the fire and struggled frantically to escape the locked and force-flooded death chamber.

Marines and sailors caught in their sleep in the berthing compartments were in various poses. Some apparently had been suffocated without ever coming to consciousness, others looked horrified or frantic, and some appeared to have been retching and choking when death came, their eyes bulging.

During the day, each body was brought to the main deck, placed into a body bag, and sent to the ship's freezer for storage. As evening fell on the *Newport News*, she was making cruising speed in the direction of Subic Bay. The ship looked normal in all respects with the exception of the number two turret, which was still cranked outboard, its barrels raised to the angle they held in their last salvo. The center barrel, which weighed nearly ten tons, hung precariously from its liner. The outer casing had been blown free of its connection to the breach. Damage control crews had chained and fastened cinches to it to prevent it from falling onto the main deck.

Back of turret two after October 1 explosion

Black soot and charred paint surrounded the breach and the six-inch thick steel doors on the back of the turret. The rubber "boot" surrounding the barrel where it joined to the forward surface of the turret was melted and charred. The mechanical workings of the turret had been burned too badly to perform their task, and the huge steel mass could not be rotated back to its centerline position. It was a gruesome image of death, lying agape and out of place with the rest of the ship's lines.

Air conditioning had been shut down to the forward part of the ship because of breaks in the Freon lines, and Radio One got up to a hot ninety-five degrees as the ship made its way across the Philippine Sea. Ray and Mike had been split to cover the two twelve-hour watches per day. Others of the comm crew were rescheduled to fill in the places of the eight members of CR Division who were evacuated to hospitals by helicopter. Tactical communications were dropped as the ship departed the gun line, but the immense volume of logistics and support traffic needed to accommodate the ship's movement back to Subic for repair and assessment kept the Teletype Center humming. Added to that was the flurry of "class easy" traffic, the personal telegram messages each member of the crew was anxious to send to their loved ones to let them know they had survived.

It was a major news event on October 2, 1972 that the heavy cruiser *USS Newport News* had experienced an onboard explosion while shooting a support mission in North Vietnam. Hundreds of concerned families sent telegrams of inquiry, which further hampered the now clogged communications center.

The ship arrived at Subic on the 3rd and remained in port for repairs and an investigation of the damage. It would take until the 19th of October before the ship was repaired and deemed fit for service once more. Turret two was rotated back to the centerline position, its center gun removed, and a steel plate bolted to the opening. The turret was never used again, which meant *Thunder* had lost one-third of its main battery punch.

Exploded gun detached from turret

Turret two with missing gun

Debauchery ran rampant among the crew of *Thunder* for the sixteen days they were sequestered in Subic. The men drank to oblivion often; officers and staff discouraged none of this activity. For the most part the Navy actually tried to provide a stress release for the crew. There were forays out to Granby Island, a recreational area reserved for R&R activities, which included picnics, cook outs, and beer blasts centered around softball, basketball, and soccer games. The island was a calming, tropical paradise several miles removed from the mainland. The Government recreational facilities had been developed there and used for years to help soldiers and sailors "decompress" or unwind from their combat experiences.

The usual fair of activities in Olongapo City abounded, and *Thunder*'s crew was now an experienced group around the clubs and brothels.

Bobby and Ray hung out together, and it seemed to Ray that his friend was beginning to put away his obsession with Lisa. Bobby had adapted the "fuck it" attitude of surrender to the inevitable.

"Fuck it, Ray, there's nothing worth worrying about anymore. I'm just gonna have all the fun and booze and drugs I can handle and forget about the world, fucking Vietnam, and everything else in life. I'm gonna live for today, for this moment only, nothing else."

"That's the spirit Bobby Boy, no fuckin' sense in thinking about anything. Just get numb and laid and wake up tomorrow and do it all over again. Shit, we could be as dead as those gunners mates and Marines in another couple of weeks. Piss on it." They clanged their shot glasses together and slammed the bourbon down, quickly washing it back with a long pull on their mugs of beer.

The ship arrived back in Military Region One on October 23 and began the same old routine, shooting support missions from her remaining six eight-inch barrels. There was one significant difference.

When the salvos went out this time, many of the men blinked and grimaced, and prayed the guns would not explode again.

Subtle affects could be seen among some of the crewmembers. Bobby began to stutter and Ray's left eyelid twitched involuntarily. There were many long faces, there were very few jokes, and the banter the young men had earlier taken into battle with them had fallen away. Their faces looked serious, sometimes pathetic. Tempers were short and fights broke out over the slightest provocation. They were tired, they were worn out, and they were demoralized.

Chapter 22

Return to Love

For the remainder of October and November the *Newport News* and her crew fired missions in MR1. There were no more night raids with Task Unit 77.1. Message traffic between *Thunder*'s captain and Commander Seventh Fleet indicated that Zartman felt skeptical of the operational readiness of his ship and her crew with regard to the high stress environment of the Linebacker Strikes.

There were many more zombie-faced sailors and officers, and morale continued to degrade as the long periods of slow and continual pounding of targets in Quang Tri Province progressed. Many of the crew felt the ship was doomed and that another disaster was destined to occur. Even Commander Stroud, who had seldom shown any sign of emotion, seemed depressed and more quiet than ever, and Ray wondered how Chief Yerks would have seemed had he not left them in the midst of their warrior frenzy.

There were two more brief periods of R&R in Subic Bay, and when November 29 came the ship had returned there for maintenance and upkeep once more. By this time the crew was extremely weary. Rumors abounded that the ship would be held captive here in the Seventh Fleet for as long as the war lasted. Sailors speculated that materials and technicians would be shipped to Subic to repair turret two so the ship could again become the central element of the strike force up north. The captain had announced to the crew that the ship's schedule had been extended indefinitely. This fact seemed to substantiate the rumors that *Thunder* would be repaired and permanently transferred to the Seventh Fleet.

Many of the sailors were angry, tired of the war, and appalled that the military could indefinitely keep them in this limbo-like existence of near-death. The dark humor and sarcasm of a few months earlier reached new levels of contempt and hopelessness. The men even saw Captain Zartman as an ogre, a part of the system that had no sympathy for the men who had sacrificed their comfort and sanity for this seemingly hopeless war.

"We're nothing but warm bodies," men would say, "meaningless and expendable to those we serve. They have no respect for our needs and no concern about whether we ever see our families again. We thought Zartman had balls, but he won't even stand up to the brass—what a kiss-ass."

In fact, Captain Zartman and his staff were making every effort to convince the Seventh Fleet Commander that the crew was battle weary and hovering on the verge of dangerous because of their rapidly deteriorating morale.

On the 1st of December the ship again departed Subic after a two-day maintenance period. Her orders were to return to Vietnam. Twelve sailors decided they were not going back to the war zone and did not report aboard for the departure. The ship steamed out of the mouth of Subic Bay Harbor and once again took a course straight for the coast of Vietnam.

Four hours out of port, as the great cruiser began a sharp turn to the South, the captain's voice came over the speakers: "This is the captain speaking. I know many of you are feeling pretty low right now, and I do not blame you for feeling that way. This has been a long and arduous deployment with significant losses for all of us. So it is with the hope of cheering you up that I make the following report to you. Commander Seventh Fleet has released us from further commitments in this part of the world and, as I speak, the ship is coming around to a course which will take us back to Norfolk, hopefully by Christmas. I want to thank you all for the great sacrifices you've made in the past eight months, and extend my hopes that you will all have a very joyous Christmas and reunion with your families. Now let's get the hell out of here before they change their minds."

A unified roar of jubilation permeated every space of the ship. In seconds, the long faces and caustic remarks turned to smiles and elation. A cloud of ominous foreboding lifted and the sun streamed through almost as if it penetrated the heavy steel of the cruiser. They were going home.

Within hours the word had been passed throughout the ship that all hands would stand down and observe "Holiday Routine." With the exception of those whose task it was to sail the ship back home, the plan for the remainder of the cruise was leisure. No uniform dress code need be kept with the exception of on-deck personnel interacting with the refueling and supply ships. Now all the men had to do was pass the time required to transit the Pacific, go through the Panama Canal, and sail back up the east coast.

Many of the crewmembers responded immediately, pouring out onto the weather decks clothed in cut-off shorts and bare feet. The smooth teak wood decks felt soothing, as if providing confirmation that their plight was over. Card games and impromptu circles of buddies scattered willy-nilly about the main deck sprang up. Occasionally, after sunset, these would turn into pot-smoking circles. The officers simply looked the other way.

Whatever behavior the crew deemed appropriate was permissible, as long as it did not present any danger or overtly subversive attitudes. Without exception they were all incredibly thankful to be out of the war zone and heading home. Officers and enlisted men alike felt rejuvenated and full of hope for the first time in months.

Their morale improved by great measure. Immediately, joking and cajoling that had not been experienced in some time began to overtake the sullen attitudes that had become more commonplace.

For CR Division, all communications were curtailed with the exception of those needed to coordinate the movement of *Thunder* back to her home. The members who had suffered smoke inhalations in the October explosion had all returned with clean bills of health. Radio silence was observed as much as possible in order to keep Southeast Asia from learning that the heavy cruiser was absent. This was the same reason the crew had not been informed of their impending return before leaving Subic.

The twelve men who remained behind had chosen the wrong time to desert, had they stayed aboard they would have been elated to learn the truth with the rest of the crew, but their fear and anxiety had prevented that. Captain Zartman sent his wishes to the Commander of Subic Bay Naval Base and Commander Seventh Fleet that the Navy would not exercise its most stringent penalty rulings for these men. Though it was written in the Uniform Code of Military Justice that deserters in time of war could be subject to the death penalty, the absence of a declared war in Vietnam and the understanding of a benevolent commander would serve to soften their plight. He did suggest, however, that they were no longer considered members of his crew and he would not interfere with the Navy's decision to penalize them.

Letter writing became the number one objective of all hands; most of them hoped that the letters would somehow be allowed to get to their relatives and friends in time for them to greet them upon arrival in Norfolk.

As it happened, that was the case. The ship pulled into pier seven at NOB Norfolk the afternoon of December 24, 1972 in the presence of nearly 5,000 anxious relatives, friends, and well-wishers waiting on the pier. Simultaneously, there were peace demonstrations going on at the main gate of the Naval Base to deride the efforts of the returning men, the Navy, and the U.S. Government.

The sailors lined the lifelines of the main deck and weather decks in their dress blue uniforms as mighty *Thunder* slid quietly to her moorings with the aid of tugboats. A Navy band played Sousa Marches and traditional military music as mooring lines were made fast and gangplanks were put in place. The press was present and photographer's flash packs illuminated the area like fireworks in the late afternoon shadows. Thousands of joyous greeters released helium balloons, streamers, and confetti while the ship's crew began to disembark and mingle with the crowd.

Sailors lining the decks of Newport News *as she sails into Norfolk harbor*

Home crowd waiting for the sailors

Ray stood at quarters with the rest of CR Division on the port side outboard promenade, aft of the flag bridge, one deck above the main deck and high above the crowd on the pier. The crewmembers were released a section at a time from their stations, a process that seemed to take forever. Ray searched the crowd continually, frantically scanning to recognize the beautiful young face he had longed to see for so long. It had been nine months since he had seen her, and, in that time, the entire world had changed around him. *Where is she?* he thought. *Did she stay away? Is there something wrong? Maybe it's over between us and she couldn't tell me, maybe she isn't coming. Maybe it's really over.*

Time seemed to stand still, as it had in those harrowing moments in combat. Ray grew more anxious, he was feeling frantic. The crowd was so dense it covered the entire pier. It was one huge mass of faces and waving arms and excited shouts. The streaming line of sailors and officers poured faster and faster off the gangplanks. Swirls of movement flowed through the masses on the pier when long separated Servicemen and their loved ones reacted in sudden recognition, involuntarily lunging and grasping to make contact and embrace at long last.

The sailors were headed down the main deck now, slowly crowding toward the after-gangplank. They packed in closer and closer like an excited crowd pressing the gates of a sports arena to see a rock concert. Ray still did not see a familiar face. His heart was beginning to sink. He felt there was something terribly wrong. Had he misread the letters? Was there a last minute change? *Mom, Dad, Cynthia, where are you? I can't believe I can't find you out there,* he said to himself.

Suddenly he heard his name, very faintly above the crowd, in a high-pitched voice. He caught a glimpse of a frantically waving hand with a white handkerchief in it. He focused on the hand, then he saw the familiar face. It was Betty Fancher, a close family friend, and she was pushing through the crowd toward the gangplank. Betty was a little taller than average height and a fit looking fifty-year-old woman with dark brown hair. She was wearing a plaid scarf and black winter coat, and it looked like she was holding on to someone else and pulling him or her through the crowd, but Ray couldn't make out the other person. Then he saw there were others behind following closely, and he made out his father's Fedora hat. His heart beat faster. Like an eagle whose watchful eye had been drawn to a faint movement in the distance, Ray remained transfixed on the four partially obscured figures attempting to make progress through the crowd. Then he glimpsed a brief image of the face he was looking for. His heart raced, he strained against the sailors in front of him, and pushed involuntarily against them. He felt choked and flushed with a surge of excitement. Involuntarily his mouth shaped the word and made the sound.

"Cynthia! Cynthia!" he yelled as he continued to press forward. He shot a hand up and waved at her. From twenty yards away he could see the look of recognition in her eyes as she waved back and pointed up at the huge ship. Ray's mom was right behind her, and Cynthia was pulling her with one hand and pointing with the other as the four of them, Ray's father in the rear and Betty still leading in front, pressed through the excited crowd. They made their way to the edge of the pier, as close as they could get to the gangplank before stopping ten yards from where Ray was still working his way toward the gangplank. They could see one another clearly now, all of them had tears of joy streaming down their cheeks. They waved and shouted and smiled with joy, reaching out toward one another.

It was another excruciatingly long five minutes before the sailors crowding off the gangplank had dispersed sufficiently for Ray to make it to his waiting parents and his beautiful fiancée. By now the entire pier was crowded to capacity with people. The congestion was so great that Shore Patrol officers were trying ever so respectfully to move them all off the pier and onto the surrounding roadways and parking areas to accommodate the passage of those still trying to disembark. Crewmembers aboard the surrounding ships at the Naval Base were outside on their weather decks observing the joyous calamity of this event.

Finally, Ray and his fiancée came together and embraced. Cynthia and Ray held each other so close it felt like they were fused together, never to be separated again. They kissed and hugged and cried and held each other as Ray's parents and their friend encircled them, placing their arms around the couple's necks and shoulders. There were kisses and hugs for everyone as the five of them exchanged expressions of love and joy while unconsciously moving with the gentle flow of the masses toward the shoreward end of the pier.

In twenty-five minutes they were warm and cozy in Ray's parents' Chrysler, moving ever-so-slowly with the mass of log-jammed traffic exiting the Naval Base. Ray and Cynthia sat in the rear seat with Betty, though they were so engulfed in the rapture of each other's presence it was hard for them to notice anything else. Ray's father drove them all to the hotel in Oceanview where they had reserved two rooms for the night. They spent one hour or so visiting in the two-room suite before walking to the restaurant across the street for dinner.

After a delicious, celebratory meal of festive, holiday proportions, Ray and Cynthia took a long walk along the sandy dunes in the now deserted off-season winter chill of the Virginia shore. It was Christmas Eve. They were far away from their homes, but they were together again. They were all alone on the beach in the chilly wind. In the distance they could hear the crashing surf. There was a bright yellow quarter-moon together with a few twinkling stars, a black sea, and an occasional puffy cloud illuminated by the moonlight. They talked, they held hands, they kissed, and they beamed with joy at each other.

Cynthia was so beautiful. Ray could not take his eyes off her. Her long, wavy, chestnut brown hair fell in curls around her shoulders. Her big, beautiful eyes seemed to change from hazel to light green in the light as they walked from the shadowy darkness into the faint illumination of streetlights and Christmas decorations in the quiet seaside community. She had long curled eyelashes and gently arching brows that contrasted with her mid-winter, alabaster complexion. Just a hint of makeup accented her prominent cheekbones and soft, creamy facial contours. Plush, moist, subtly-glossed lips parted to reveal pearly white teeth as she smiled and spoke soft, sweet words of affection. They paused often to embrace and kiss. More and more passionately their desires mounted as they strolled farther out into the open expanse of sandy beach. She had abundant, firm breasts that pressed against Ray's chest through the heavy winter coats they both wore. Cynthia's beautifully proportioned, shapely body was warm and building with subtle energy as they lingered longer and more contently with each successive embrace. *She seemed more mature than her eighteen years*, Ray thought, *and at the same time even younger and more innocent than he had remembered her*.

"You are so very beautiful, and I love you so very much. I've missed you like I never thought possible," Ray said as he stroked her face gently with three fingers and then fondled the curl of soft hair lying against her cheek.

"Oh my love," she began as the tears once again streamed from her eyes, "I love you so much, I was so afraid I would never see you again. I never want to be away from you again." Ray brushed the tears from her cheeks with a finger and kissed her tenderly, tasting the saltiness of her tears and the sweetness of her tongue and lips. They lingered there for a long, warm, engulfing, wonderful moment.

They made love on the beach in the cold sand and the black night, with the chilly wind swirling around their naked skin. They pulled their coats and clothes around them and held each other tightly inside the drafty cocoon of garments. Emotional comfort fended off the chill, their love keeping them warm. They lay there together for an eternity and touched and kissed and fondled each other's smooth skin and firm flesh. They remained engulfed in euphoric bliss; it seemed like time stood still for them.

When they returned to the hotel, the lights were off in the adjacent room, and the door between them had been locked. They were puzzled at first, but as the obvious conclusion occurred to them, they felt blessed to have the opportunity to be alone in pure love and ecstasy for the rest of the night.

Morning came with bright sunlight flickering through the slits of gently fluttering drapes that moved with the breeze coming through the partially opened window next to their bed. There was a soft rapping on the door from the adjacent room and Betty's voice spoke softly, "Are you two up in there? We're getting ready to go to breakfast. Do you want to join us?"

"We'll be right there," Ray answered. "Give us a few minutes, we'll meet you in the restaurant."

Ray and Cynthia arose and dressed feeling strangely mindful that his parents and Betty were fully aware they had slept together. Was it all right? After all, the others had gone to sleep and left them a room to themselves. What would they think?

They all ate breakfast together, and everything seemed fairly normal though Ray and Cynthia both felt a little uneasy. At first it seemed like everyone was a little quieter than usual, but before long conversations developed, the tension eased, and the joy of reunion returned to them all.

They drove home to Pennsylvania that Christmas Day, and Ray and Cynthia and their families had a wonderful and joyous holiday. Ray took thirty days leave from the Navy, and he and Cynthia spent as much of that time as they could celebrating their reunion, visiting with their friends, and rekindling their long set aside relationship. Thankfully, their love had survived.

Ray and Cynthia, 1977

My Story

I did not write *Thunder in the Night* until thirty years after my military service. It was a part of my life that would not integrate and behave, as a good little memory should. I went through much pain and turmoil before reaching the point where I could write the story. I finally decided to write in the third person in order to maintain separation between the young sailor in the story and the Ray Kopp of today. I found this a milder way of dealing with my emotions about the deaths of Brian and my shipmates, the events of 1972, and the Vietnam Era in general. My struggle with the Vietnam experience was long, but it taught me a great deal.

As I began *Thunder in the Night*, I realized I needed to do much research for the book and knew the information I needed would be difficult to obtain. There was precious little ever written about the actions of my Task Unit in Vietnam; a few accounts of Aircraft Carrier operations, Swift Boats, Riverine Patrols and SEALs were all I could unearth on the topic of naval warfare in Southeast Asia. The general perception of naval ships during the Vietnam War was that they languished off shore, lobbing shells into places where ground forces called for support. By and large that was the case, but not always. There was but one brief account in official Navy historical records of the combat described in my book. I knew the reason these had been omitted…there was no interest in the final U.S. offensive of the war. The world was sick of the war in Vietnam, and details of these operations were unpopular. It was also feared these operations would be viewed as political mistakes.

Upon returning home, those of us who had taken part in the final efforts to "Vietnamize" the war soon came to realize that the narratives of our experiences were not appreciated. A huge dichotomy began to grow within us as we realized there was an intentional effort to leave no record of the hardest thing we had ever done in our lives. We were advised to wear neither our uniforms nor the campaign ribbons we had earned. Even more than when we had left for Vietnam, it was extremely unpopular to be connected with the military.

From the time I was a child, I had intended to be a career serviceman and spent much time working toward that goal. When my separation date grew near, the Navy suggested a number of opportunities to better myself if I chose to re-enlist. I was offered a chance to enroll in a Navy educational program called NECEP that would send me to college to earn a degree. Assuming I graduated from college, I would receive a commission as a lieutenant. This was extremely attractive to me, but after Vietnam I was ultimately unable to choose this path. My faith in what I was doing, what I had done, and what I was capable of had been severely shaken upon returning home. Many of my peers in the civilian world seemed to despise the military—and even the United States itself—because of their perceptions of the Vietnam War. As had been the case with the first "Forgotten War" in Korea, we found ourselves trying to put the past and our connection to the War behind us as though it was a criminal record.

On April 30 1975, nearly two years after my release from active service, I awoke in a cold, dank, one-room apartment in a hung-over stupor. There was music blaring from my stereo system. Just as I awoke, the news came on and reported that Saigon had fallen and the North Vietnamese had conquered the South Vietnamese Government. I wept. I had great feelings of guilt. I had recurring thoughts of what it was like to lose my best friend, Brian. I had the memory that the command I had been a part of had taken thousands of lives from soldiers and defenders of North Vietnam. I was aware of the collateral casualties in the civilian population. Now it felt like it had all been for nothing. It was gut wrenching to me.

I questioned my own morality and felt guilt that I had survived when so many others had been killed. I had already begun to encounter people who denigrated and belittled Vietnam veterans and the war in general. Now I became reclusive, introverted, and unresponsive to the needs of others; a self-condemned social outcast. Vietnam stayed in the recesses of my mind for decades.

In 1985 I found myself in a crowded bar room at Veterans of Foreign Wars Post 6223. I often sought the company of veterans of other wars and had a strong desire to be accepted by them. World War II veterans were among my greatest heroes; they had given me the values and respect I held for all U.S. servicemen. On this particular night, one of these World War II veterans leaned over and asked what war I had fought in. I was a new member of the VFW and knew that the

VFW did not initially accept us as members. I also knew that when they finally did decide to admit us, many members disagreed with the decision. A bit frightened of the response I might receive, I leaned toward the gentleman and sheepishly responded, "Vietnam." The man proceeded to dress me down in front of the entire Friday night crowd. He called me every name in the book, including, "doper," "druggie," and "failure," while adding a great number of expletives along the way. There it was; I had been accosted by a man from the very generation of my greatest heroes. I left the VFW, trying to retain my dignity by covering my face so no one could see the tears flowing down my cheeks. After this experience, I became secretive with respect to my service history. When people asked if I served during Vietnam, I simply said "yes" without adding any details.

I had undergone long, periods of deep depression since my mid- and late-twenties, but I did not actually associate them with my wartime experiences. I had done a pretty good job of burying these things deep within me. I had my share of sleepless nights and periods of pity and self-absorption but didn't everybody? The heavy drinking to oblivion that had started in Subic Bay became my sanctuary. With alcohol and marijuana, I could get myself into an altered state that would dull the lows and mellow my spirit. This "worked" for many years.

There is a phrase among those in "recovery programs" upon which the first step of the 12-step process is based, and it has to do with one's powerlessness over a substance and the unmanageability of one's life. I, however, was never convinced I was powerless over anything or that my life was ever unmanageable. It was my chosen self-proof that if I could continue to partake of my "recreational activities" and still show up for work most of the time, there was nothing wrong with the way I was living. I subscribed to the idea that those who worked hard were entitled to play hard when the work was done.

This abuse of substances continued until the age of forty without serious consequences. I became what is referred to as a "functional" alcoholic. (I must take a moment here to explain that I am not suggesting my alcoholism was only a result of the war in Vietnam or the experiences I went through during my military service; I believe I would probably have been an alcoholic whatever the circumstances of my life. I do believe, however, that the mood swings, depression, anger, and resentment pent-up within me gave me a very good excuse for being a drunk.) As a functioning alcoholic, I did quite well in my career endeavors, despite occasional difficulties with authority figures and employers. But, again, "unmanageability" was not in my vocabulary. I was stubbornly convinced that anything short of what I had felt in combat was in no way threatening. In short, after knowing the chaos and futility of war, nothing in the civilized world posed a threat to me.

Then, in 1986, the Aerospace firm I was employed in for nearly thirteen years was taken over. Over the next four years I slowly lost hold of the only important career opportunity I ever had. In the end of 1990, a group of us were unceremoniously herded into a conference room, stripped of our government security clearances, debriefed, and terminated. The shock of losing my identity as a designer in Aerospace electronics was devastating. I began a long process of trying to re-establish myself in that field, but it was not to be. At the age of forty, with only a portion of my college education completed, I was not in the running in such a competitive field.

The next nine years were a calamity. First I decided to continue my college degree program and started school full time. I had divorced my second wife and remarried for a third time. The substance abuse continued. Then came the advent of the 1991 Gulf War. I found myself caught up in intense controversy and emotional turmoil over current events. The feelings of demoralization over my career loss, the stresses of engineering school, and the haunting and recurring memories of my time in Southeast Asia began to take control of my life. I walked out of classes one day never to return. By the end of the year, I was at a place where I could no longer go on. I was broken in heart and spirit, and, for the first time, felt suicidal.

I spent the next few years of my life trying to regain some degree of normalcy. I tried and failed in five separate occupational endeavors, each time finding that any type of stressful circumstances would make me shut down. I would become deeply emotionally disturbed and withdraw to a secluded place, trembling with anxiety and fear. I had totally inappropriate responses to mildly disturbing situations. I went into treatment for substance abuse three different times and experienced, at one time, over three years of abstinence from alcohol and drugs. During each period of sobriety, however, I would become more and more stressed, angry, and unstable. Then, eventually, I would reach a point where I would run away, get drunk, and fall back into my destructive routine of reality evasion. This happened time and again so that, by the autumn of 1999, the toll of my inability to face life effectively had accumulated in the loss of three marriages and two stepfamilies; three DWIs; several demolished vehicles; three periods of hospitalization due to vehicular accidents; over thirty fractures in my face, hands, ribs, and legs; and the loss of untold amounts of money.

Yet, I still did not fully believe my life was unmanageable. I was, however, *beginning* to think I might be wrong about that.

Finally, in the summer and fall of 2000, a number of life events came together and took me to a new low in mental and psychological health. I stood at the edge of life looking into the abyss and desiring a quick ticket to the hereafter. I awoke in the emergency room of the Cayuga Medical Center a few days before Thanksgiving, and was transferred to the Mental Health Unit when my physical condition was judged stable. After my stay there I was referred to the Veterans Administration. I had two appointments with a lady named Mary Fear at the Veteran's Center in Syracuse, NY. Mary said she had no doubt I was suffering the effects of Post-Traumatic Stress Disorder (PTSD) related to my experiences in Vietnam, and that I was obviously chemically dependent. The "good news" she said, was that both were treatable and that I was not alone; the majority of combat PTSD sufferers were also chemically dependent. Then she said something I had never heard before—she told me she was not surprised I had experienced so many failed attempts to stay sober. Mary believed it was nearly impossible for anyone who was suffering from both PTSD and chemical dependency to recover from either without simultaneous treatment for both.

In January of 2001, I began the long road back to normalcy. I first went to a domiciliary complex in the VA Healthcare System, and then went on to continuing treatment and therapy. As I learned more about my emotional condition, I was better able to separate my feelings from the real facts and memories of my combat experiences. I was able to write *Thunder in the Night* only after prolonged periods of treatment from the VA as well as a private counseling clinic in Binghamton, NY[1]. Using a method called Bonding Psychotherapy and a technique called EMDR, I could recover enough to write of my experiences in Vietnam.

Over the last four years, I have returned to a state of health mentally and physically that I have not had in my adult life. I tell many today I am in the best condition I have been in since I was seventeen years old, and I mean it. By the grace of God, the VA, and the help of

---

[1] Using a method called Bonding Psychotherapy and a technique called EMDR, George was able to help me recover enough to write of my experiences in Vietnam. Mr. Rynick, who holds a Masters of Divinity and numerous well-earned accreditation and certifications in different methods of psychotherapy, has become a dear friend, mentor, and counselor to me and many others. He holds the title of teaching fellow and lifetime honorary President in the International Society of Bonding Psychotherapy. The Society of Bonding Psychotherapy can be accessed at the following website: http://www.bondingpsychotherapy.com

people in two fellowships involved with recovery, I am now the person I could have been all those years ago.

* * *

I need to say what I feel about our present day national disunity in terms of what I have learned from a lifetime of difficulty. **We must always support our service men and women with everything we have.** It is not appropriate to demonstrate against our people in uniform *or their efforts*. These selfless patriots, who go in harm's way to support the interests of democracy and freedom, should never be made to feel we are ungrateful for their efforts.

The time to make decisions as citizens of this country is at election time. Taking aim at our own government with simplistic themes like "war is wrong" solves no problems; instead it creates disunity and dissent. The effects of these are deeply felt by those who serve the cause abroad. To protest the war is to protest the soldier; there is no way to separate one from the other.

If one looks at the documented and historical record, and particularly at the documents signed in the Paris Peace Accord of 1973, it is clear that the Vietnam War was won and ended with the word of the North Vietnamese not to interfere militarily in the south. *Because of rampant disunity among the people of this country* and the fall from grace of the Nixon Administration due to Watergate, the U.S. was unable to make those agreements last. Extreme pressures imposed on our government to leave Vietnam nullified the end result and made the deaths of 58,000 American soldiers a senseless tragedy. That, to me, is unforgivable. Many would say those losses are proof that war is wrong; that it is never the answer. Agreed, war should never be a choice when there are valid alternatives, and the government of this country has always operated on that premise. No administration, knowing the realities of war, would undertake it as anything but a last resort. Moreover, when our elected officials send the military to fight against tyranny and terrorism and in defense of democracy, it is their duty to do so.

Today, those in the Armed Forces voluntarily accept the responsibility to go. They cannot choose whether or not they wish to participate—it is their commitment. Yet today among the military, there is nearly unanimous support for the war on terrorism and the Bush administration.

The deaths of 58,000 Americans are not the greatest tragedy of the Vietnam Era. The estimated *four million casualties* among the

Vietnamese, Laotian, and Cambodian people *together with* our military losses are the horrific result of our loss of unity then. At least half of those occurred in the aftermath when we left Southeast Asia. The tyrannical methods of the Communists in Vietnam and elsewhere were well reported. The Communist Vietnamese were never liberators or nationalists. They, like the North Koreans, were agenda Communists bolstered by the Soviets and Chinese to further their common cause of Communism in the guise of Marxist Socialism.

Those of us who fought in Southeast Asia believed we were fighting to free an oppressed people from tyranny. Anti-American factions here and abroad succeeded in bringing that cause into question. These leftist factions spouted an array of alternative motives for that war, none of which was ever validated. Vietnam was said to have vast mineral resources and untapped, offshore oil reserves. Some claimed it was the key to the Orient, a tropical paradise to be exploited for recreational purposes. It was said to have something the U.S. wanted to possess. If these claims had been true, Vietnam would be a wealthy nation today; instead it has fallen deeper into economic collapse.

Now, some politicians and media manipulators are inciting controversy over the Iraq War. They use the same twisted reasoning of the Vietnam era. They spew ulterior motives and suggest we are exploiting Iraq because of oil and resources, that we are fighting a war against Islam, that we are allied with Israel to control the Middle East. According to them there are no proofs of Iraq's affiliation with terrorism or weapons of mass destruction. They would have us believe lack of evidence is proof those things never existed.

There seem to be other proofs they are missing. For example, what about the proof that Saddam Hussein *himself* was a weapon of mass destruction? He and his sons did personally torture and murder people. Hussein used chemical weapons on the Kurds, shot Scud missiles indiscriminately into Israel, set fire to the oil wells in Kuwait, and held his nation in the grip of extreme oppression. Does anyone see anything wrong with those acts of tyranny?

The optimistic belief that we humans have evolved beyond war is, sadly, not true. It is a noble aspiration, but simply false. As a leader of democracy and freedom, America has the responsibility to help those who do not have basic human rights. Sometimes this means fighting against those who deny those rights, especially the perpetrators of terrorist acts against innocent people. It is that simple, there are no ulterior motives.

The intense emotion over U.S. foreign policy today is unlike anything I have seen since the Vietnam War. This type of disunity caused our failure in Vietnam and it can do the same to our military efforts now and in the future. Despite the efforts of many to draw parallels between Vietnam and Iraq, the following is the only one I see: The Vietnam War began with solid national unity, and that unity dwindled as time dragged on. That war has remained infamous as the only war America lost. It is still misunderstood by many, but it taught us many lessons. One of the most important lessons *should have been*: **do not make the same mistakes**. Losing our national unity now could very well result in losses in Afghanistan, Iraq, and—in a larger sense—the war against terrorism. We need to stick together and see this effort through to the end unless we wish to have another Vietnam.

In times of war, demonstrations against our foreign policies only demoralize our troops and create opposition among our citizens. If well-meaning Americans in the 1940s had derailed the military and industrial machine that conquered Nazi Germany and Imperialist Japan, or if we had lost the Cold War, the world would be much different today; it would be dominated by fascism and tyranny. There would be little freedom for anyone. Without our resolve to fight tyranny to the end, this country and what it stands for will disappear.

We will not remain free unless we recognize tyranny and have the courage and resolve to fight it. The cause of freedom has always been, and still is, a primary objective in the battle of good against evil. **The noblest cause of freedom is to set others free.**

Freedom *is* worth fighting for, and fighting a war takes unity.

Raymond S. Kopp

Epilogue

She had fired over 50,000 rounds of eight- and five-inch artillery into North Vietnam, and she had taken on the order of 2,000 rounds of counter battery from the enemy. She and her crew had conducted sixty-eight offensive strike raids against North Vietnam and hundreds of support missions to the South. She looked war weary; her once "spit and polish" appearance as a flagship had been replaced with a rusty, shrapnel-pocked hulk. The ravages of combat were apparent. During the deployment, the Heavy Cruiser *USS Newport News* had lost a total of twenty-two members of her crew, one to a forklift accident on the way to Vietnam, one to a man overboard incident, and twenty to the explosion and fire of October 1. It is to those fine, young men that this book is humbly dedicated.

From December 18 to December 30, 1972 the U.S. conducted the second phase of Operation Linebacker, known as Linebacker II. Later known as the "Christmas Bombings," Linebacker II was the largest and most intensified bombing campaign of the Vietnam War. Made possible in part by the elimination of a significant number of surface-to-air missile sites and coastal defense artillery positions during the Linebacker I phase, its intent was to break the resolve of the North Vietnamese and bring them to the peace table in Paris from a position of submission. It worked. On January 17, 1973 all parties involved signed the Paris Peace Accord and hostilities in Vietnam ceased.

At this point the U.S. Government felt it had achieved its objectives in Southeast Asia and, within a few months, had withdrawn all personnel, dismantled its bases, and cleared the mines from North Vietnamese waterways. The Vietnam War was over. By extricating itself from the Indochina quagmire, the last steps toward the Vietnamization of the war had been implemented. The agreement called for the North and South to end hostilities and seek a political resolution to their differences, and it further restricted either of their governments from intervening in the governments of Laos and Cambodia. Such was agreed on jointly by the Democratic Republic of

Vietnam, the United States, the People's Republic of China, the Republic of France, the Union of Soviet Socialist Republics, the United Kingdom, and the Secretary General of the United Nations.

After the U.S. withdrawal, the United States became engulfed in a new debacle which would come to be known as the Watergate Scandal, and all memories of the war in Vietnam would soon fade from the consciousness of its citizens. There was a strong desire to forget about Vietnam.

By April of 1975, the "peaceful people of the Democratic Republic of Vietnam" had rebuilt their military machine and rearmed their workingman's army to the point where the initial plan of overtaking the south was again viable. And overtake they did. It has been estimated that between 1975 and 1979 the casualties of the communist takeover of South Vietnam, along with the communist backed siege of Cambodia and Laos, amounted to the deaths of between two and four million more people.

The controversy over the war in Vietnam has been and continues to be one of the greatest points of contention in the military history of the United States. Of the many stories and tributes written to date, the vast majority paint a picture of rice patties and jungles, ambushes and booby traps, and grunts slogging through the mud and mire that has come to be known as the Vietnam experience. My purpose in putting together this book was to write the untold story of the thousands of men who participated in that conflict in an experience that was quite apart from the "normal" Vietnam image. In doing so, I mean no disrespect to anyone in any phase or region of the quagmire that came to be known as the war we lost.

Every veteran I have known and thousands I have never met, including those in any conflict anywhere in the world, who has done nothing more than "show up" to defend his/her country and the principles in which he/she believes has earned the status of hero and patriot in my humble opinion. And to those who disagree, I am one who can honestly say I have put my life on the line to defend your right to do so.

Memories being what they are and time having its influence upon them, I make no claim as to the precise accuracy of events portrayed in this book. I have worked hard to be as honest and accurate as I can. I invite the reader to examine the public record of the activities of the military commands involved. My source for the chronological sequence of my book is the ship's log from the Heavy Cruiser, *USS Newport News CA-148*. It can be viewed in its entirety and with greater detail at the following web page:

http://www.uss-newport-news.com/hist/may.htm

These web pages also include descriptions of operations conducted during this period.
http://www.history.navy.mil/seairland/chap4.htm
http://www.usshanson.org/haiphong.jpg

The text of the Paris Peace Accord of 1973 can be accessed at:
http://freelao.tripod.com/id87.htm

A list of violations by North Vietnam, brought by the United States in April 1973:
http://www.aiipowmia.com/sea/ppaviolate0473.html

For news stories about the fall of Saigon in April 1975:
http://news.bbc.co.uk/onthisday/hi/dates/stories/april/21/newsid_2935000/2935347.stm
http://news.bbc.co.uk/1/hi/world/asia-pacific/720724.stm

The last page of the following sight contains a press release from the new government of Vietnam, which was printed in the Agence France Presse (French Press Agency) regarding casualties of the Vietnam War:
http://www.rjsmith.com/kia_tbl.html

* * *

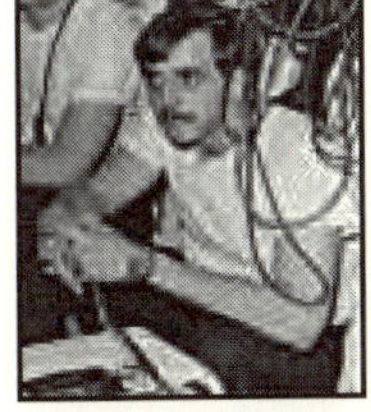

Ray and Cynthia continued the relationship that had been put on hold by the events of the summer of 1972. They married in 1976, but divorced in 1979. Cynthia remarried a few years later and found happiness with her second husband and their two sons.

Mark (Swanny) Swanson was discharged from active duty in the Navy at the same time as Ray, September 14, 1973. Swanny died of cancer in March of 1974.

Dave Brownstead returned to college, earned a degree in fine arts and art history, became a professional artist, and now lives in San Diego, California.

Ivan (Doc) Davison returned to Geraldine, Montana upon being discharged from the Navy.

Mike Haller returned to Detroit, Michigan at the end of his enlistment.

Andy (Bird) Burdulis attended the RCA School of Broadcasting and pursued a career as a communications systems analyst for an international credit card company. He now lives in New Jersey. Don Foster left the Navy, later re-enlisted and served with the SeaBees, and then transferred to the Army and spent another sixteen years in Army Special Forces before retiring as a Master Sergeant and Special Forces Instructor.

Keith (Mac) McGiffin returned to Williamsport, Pennsylvania earned a college degree and relocated to Washington D.C. where he pursued his career endeavors. Sadly, Mac died from complications of AIDS in 1994.

Rich Reith left the Navy at the end of his enlistment and entered a career with IBM. He retired from that career and is employed as a senior consultant IT and Home Health Operations professional in Atlanta, GA. Rich was instrumental in putting together the 1972 cruise book.

Commander Joel C. Stroud continued to serve the Navy with dignity until his retirement.

When Ray left the *Newport News* with his friend Swanny for the last time on September 14, 1973, Captain Zartman, Lieutenant Eric Eisenhower, Bobby Bell, and a great number of the crew from the 1972 Vietnam Cruise were still serving aboard *Thunder*.

Captain Zartman

Lieutenant Eric Eisenhower

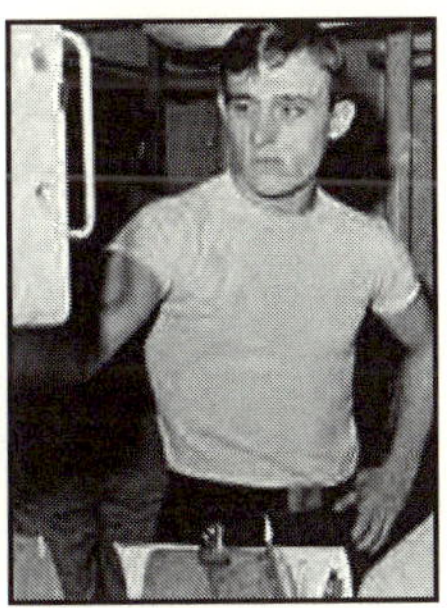

Bobby Bell

Chief Herbert Yerks retired from the Navy after a long and honorable career.

USS Newport News (CA-148) was decommissioned and retired from the Navy in 1975. She was sold for salvage in 1985. Her sole remaining sister ship, the *USS Salem* (CA-139), resides afloat at the U.S. Navy Shipbuilding Museum in Quincy, Massachusetts.